**ONLY BOOK
YOU'LL EVER
NEED**

First published 2012 by Boxtree,
an imprint of Pan Macmillan, a division of Macmillan Publishers Limited
Pan Macmillan, 20 New Wharf Road, London N1 9RR
Basingstoke and Oxford
Associated companies throughout the world
www.panmacmillan.com

ISBN 978-1-4472-2323-8

Photos © Shutterstock / iStockphoto / sxc.hu
Design by Alex Morris, after a concept by Estuary English
Printed and bound in Italy by Printer Trento

Visit www.panmacmillan.com to read more about all our books and to buy them. You will
also find features, author interviews and news of any author events, and you can sign up
for e-newsletters so that you're always first to hear about our new releases.

MOCK THE WEEK'S

ONLY BOOK YOU'LL EVER NEED

EWAN PHILLIPS, DAN PATTERSON, SIMON BULLIVANT,
ROB COLLEY, DAN GASTER, GED PARSONS,
GILES PILBROW, STEVE PUNT AND COLIN SWASH

CONTENTS

6 UNLIKELY LONELY HEARTS ADS

TWISTED SERIAL KILLER eager to meet potential victims. Any age. No photo required. PO Box 37.

MAN WITH BIG DICK seeks bird with massive tits.

SINGLE MUM seeks 'Raoul Moat type' for fun days out and chilled times.

LOOKING FOR A LADY PENELOPE to take to my Tracy Island for no-strings sex.

NON-DRINKING, non-smoking, Christian and gardener. NSOH.

GAY MAN WANTS COCK. Meet Me in These Toilets. 6.30, Wednesday.

TRAVEL ENTHUSIAST, man of leisure. Striking, well built. Seeks petite lady for fun nights. (Oh, OK, short, fat, unemployed trainspotter desperate for a fuck.)

SENIOR CABINET MINISTER WLTM dominatrix for cocaine and caning fests. Discretion v. important. Errm … oops, can people see this?

SINGLE WHITE FEMALE seeks someone for intense friendship, fashion advice and eventual murder.

WHAT DO I WANT? Sexual intercourse. When do I want it? At the first mutually convenient juncture, I suppose.

MAN, 60, beautifully dressed, Barbra Streisand fan, seeks woman with interest in interior design, watching old films and tiny dogs. Can I just underline the word 'woman' in this ad?

YOU: beautiful woman who loves short, fat, balding, traffic warden. Me: 5'5", 16-stone dreamer.

PREMIERSHIP FOOTBALLER seeks beautiful young woman to live life of unimaginable luxury whilst I continue to shag prostitutes, run up massive gambling debts and descend into violent alcoholism.

COWARDLY SUICIDE BOMBER WLTM 72 virgins so I don't actually have to do the whole blowy-uppy bit.

DIVORCEE, 45, WLTM woman of similar age for companionship, possibly relationship. Interests? What do you want to know that for? You're all so bloody nosey. What next? Are you going to start going through my fucking phone?

PERVERT desperate to meet experimental lady for fun-filled nights in. Own cheese grater preferred.

THEY SAY 'Once you've had black, you'll never go back' so before you do, come and shag one more disappointing white loser. Email now and ask for Derek.

HIGH-RANKING POLITICIAN looking for totty for rumpy-pumpy, whiff-whaff and central London fun. Email City Hall or mayor.gov and ask for B— err sorry, 'Horace'.

RECENTLY MARRIED DUCHESS looking for sportsman, Asian playboy or military cad for traditional distraction whilst my balding husband is away with RAF.

ENGLISH WOMAN currently based in Syria and growing apart from husband. Looking for knight in shining armour to come and rescue me, hopefully someone with very good security and ideally own army/air force.

8 UNLIKELY MEDICAL LABELS

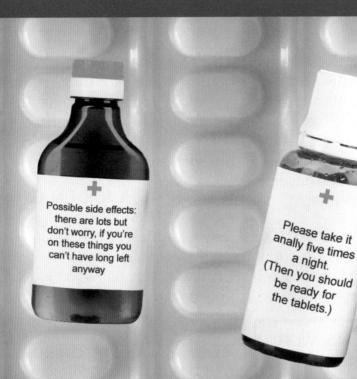

Possible side effects: there are lots but don't worry, if you're on these things you can't have long left anyway

Please take it anally five times a night. (Then you should be ready for the tablets.)

Place in water, add shallots, nutmeg and two tablespoons of Tabasco

Fuck! You haven't swallowed this have you? Arrgghhh!

Medical cannabis. For qualified patients only. Use twice a day if you can be arsed. Take with nachos and a Mars bar whilst listening to Frank Zappa

Place leech on wound. Bite down on wood. Bend head for insertion of drill

Massage in gently, starting with the hair, then work the shaft, cupping balls with other hand

Highly flammable or is it inflammable? I can never remember. Arrggh! My eyes!

Stool sample inside. If you like it, we can get you four for your kitchen

THINGS NOT TO SAY IN COURT

'If killing a man with an axe is murder, then yes, call me a murderer… Er … hang on, can I start again?'

'If this witness remembers anything, I'm suing Rohypnol.'

'I'd like to express my remorse – oh no, I'm pleading *not* guilty … Oh ducky, what am I like?'

'Erection overruled! Sorry, I don't know what came over me …'

'I can't believe you're not listening to me, a long-standing and much trusted janitor, and instead taking the word of four kids and a dog.'

'They can't be my fingerprints, I was wearing gloves.'

'This court is a charade … Three words, first word sounds like "previous".'

'If that is the law, then the law is a twat.'

'Well, she did look guilty, but she had lovely tits.'

'I look forward to being judged by twelve of my peers, by which I mean eleven pensioners and an unemployed man.'

'I sentence you to three months … sucking me off.'

'I refuse to be judged for going out with no trousers by a man in a frock and a wig.'

'I'll take my chances in Australia, thanks.'

'Yes, I admit I took my wife to Switzerland, and yes, I admit to helping her die, but the bitch had it coming to her.'

'Now jury, remember what my boys told ya.'

'Well, Your Honour, it depends how you define it. Aren't we all, in some way, guilty?'

'Which of my trials is this again?'

'I sentence you to be driven from here in a van so people can bang on it and call you a monster, and then spend the rest of your life in a maximum-security prison, receiving letters from weird, lonely women in Telford.'

'Say that again, Wiggy.'

'Does anyone mind if I jack up?'

'I demand to be tried under feudal law.'

'I swear to tell the truth, most of the truth, give or take the odd thing ...'

'Not guilty? Matching those shoes with those trousers? Send her down!'

12 UNLIKELY SCHOOL REPORT

TEACHERS' REMARKS

Dear Mr and Mrs West, Fred is working hard on the school patio. Unfortunately, the headmaster has gone missing, and is unable to congratulate him.

Dear Mr and Mrs Johnson, Boris is a very popular and intelligent boy who should go far, just as long as he isn't ever put in charge of anything complex.

DEAR MRS HAMZA, YOUNG ABU EXCELS IN WOODWORK, BUT I WORRY ABOUT HIS FLAMBOYANT USE OF THE CHAINSAW.

Dear Mr and Mrs Morgan, I'm afraid Piers is what we at this school refer to as 'a little c**t'.

Dear Mr and Mrs Suárez, Luis has had a few problems with colleagues this term but I'm sure with a quick handshake and an apology it can all be forgotten.

Dear Mr and Mrs Zuckerberg, Mark has an unfortunate habit of poking other pupils and invading their privacy. The staff do not like this.

Dear Mr and Mrs Gaga, your son is a wonderful singer and dancer.

Dear Mr and Mrs Glitter, Gary continues to get on very well with the other pupils, particularly the younger ones.

TEACHERS' REMARKS

Dear Mr and Mrs Abramovich, we are very disappointed that Roman decided to dispense with our services as his teachers. We felt we were making real progress and teaching in the style he aspired to but we hugely appreciate his generous pay-off terms.

Dear Mr and Mrs Adam, Cain and Abel really aren't getting on and I think this could spell trouble in the future.

Dear Mr and Mrs Putin, Vladimir is wonderful and I have no criticism of his behaviour. Now, could you ask him to give me my wife and children back?

Mr and Mrs Redknapp, Harry is doing well but he writes like a two-year-old.

Dear Mr and Mrs Hitler, Adolf is doing very well in science and the debating society, but spends far too much time occupying other pupils' desks.

Dear Mr and Mrs Ferguson, Alex is a hard-working pupil but he continues to annoy teachers by pointing at the bell before it's rung and then repeatedly pointing at his watch.

14 BAD THINGS TO HEAR AT YOUR

'By the way, you're adopted.'

'Right. Nobody fucking move! Keep your hands where I can see them, do as you're told and no one gets hurt.'

'OK, time for the entertainment, he was a famous singer in the 1970s ... are you ready, Gary?'

'So you pass it round and take a layer off, much like that harlot in the office your father left me for.'

'OK, well since the magician has cancelled, Sophie's father is going to give a talk on wind farms.'

'Don't eat too much cake, Olly, or you won't want your breast milk.'

'So you all go and hide and Percy the Pitbull will come and sniff you out.'

'OK, everyone settle down and I'll put the film on. It's called Schindler's List.'

'Who wants to play a drinking game?'

'Where's Joshua's dad? Well, isn't that an interesting question, Chloe? Let me get some wine and I'll tell you all about it.'

'We've got you The Woodentops; your father loved them when he was your age.'

'It's your birthday? Is it? Oh. Sorry.'

'Come on, Mr-Five-Year-Old, I think it's time you stopped using the potty now, your dad's bursting for a shit.'

'Right, let's get the toy soldiers out and we'll restage the Battle of Dettingen.'

'Now you have reached the age of five, it is time to promise your soul to the Dark Lord.'

'Here you go, Son, some weights, boxing gloves and a course of steroids. Get cracking.'

'Now, let me explain to you how me and your mummy made you ...'

16 UNLIKELY LINES FROM THE

And Adam did regret saying, 'Five years ago, that leaf would have fitted over your arse.'

The Pharaoh asked Joseph to interpret the dream where he's invisible and goes into the ladies' showers.

To Mary, hope you enjoy the book! Love Matthew, Mark, Luke and John.

You're still 2,000 words short – [Ed].

In the beginning was the Big Bang and God said, 'What the hell was that?'

And Adam said to Eve, 'Ha ha ha, looks like yours has fallen off!'

'Where are those people from?' he asked and back came the reply: 'Sodom.' And he retorted, 'No, no, I'd really like to know.'

Lot's wife did then turn into a pillar of salt and Lot was aggrieved but then thought, 'Hang on, if we have a heavy winter, she'll come in handy for the front path.'

And David did slay Goliath and there was much rejoicing until it was found that David's dad had put a massive but illegal bet on him.

If you're reading this you must be bored in a hotel room. Why not ring for a hooker instead?

After feeding everyone with loaves and fishes, Jesus said, 'Shall we just split the bill 5,000 ways?'

And lo, they were afflicted with a plague of frogs. It was the time of year for the French exchange students.

Eve noticed she was naked and was embarrassed. And Adam having a massive boner didn't help.

And Noah said, 'If it keeps raining like this, we'll have to eat the unicorns.'

Mary said to the Three Wise Men, 'Thank you for the gold and frankincense, but I'm not sure about this Olly Murs CD.'

The End – now read the first two chapters in the exciting sequel.

As Mary sat on the donkey, she realized she was about to give birth to the son of God, and should probably take off her Kiss Me Quick hat.

After Mary Magdalene had bathed the man's feet, he said, 'I actually asked for a hand job.'

And Jesus gave out the bread saying, 'This is my body,' and the wine saying, 'This is my blood.' And someone said, 'Now, is that a metaphor or do you really mean it because I think this could be important.'

The Devil appeared and tempted Jesus by saying, 'We can do all your broadband, TV and phone for only 19.99 a month.'

And Joseph said to Mary, 'Well, Jesus is alright, but I was going to go with Wayne.'

And the Israelites did lose their faith and fall to worshipping a golden idol: David Dickinson.

And David slew Goliath in a mighty upset in what was already being described as a 'David versus Goliath' contest.

18 *BAD THINGS TO SAY WHEN GIVING*

'We've run out of surgical gloves so I'm using my leather driving ones.'

'To make things easier could you do a handstand, please?'

'I'll just get the mirror and you can tell me if you're happy with that, Sir.'

'Bloody hell, what have you had up there?'

'So, would you like to go out for a drink sometime?'

'It would make things easier for me if you moaned a bit.'

'How many fingers would you be comfortable with?'

'This is my first one of these ... well, in an official capacity.'

'Brace yourself ... bang!'

'Well, it must be in here somewhere.'

'Is that cold? No? OK, now I'll try my finger.'

'Do you mind if these six young female students watch us?'

'OK, so in and out, and in and out and ...'

'I'll just put some music on.'

'Can you pretend to be my secretary and you're bending over my desk doing some filing. I'll walk in ...'

'Just close your eyes, take a deep breath and I'll insert the cactus.'

'Oh I know you, we were at Eton together in '84.'

'You're loving that, aren't you? You want it harder, don't you? You naughty boy.'

'I'll just put on the blindfold and it'll be like Pin the Tail on the Donkey.'

'Let me just give it a flick, it shouldn't hurt, just think of it like Subbuteo.'

'Actually, maybe it would be better if we pulled over onto the hard shoulder.'

'Doctor? No need to call me that, I've just come to fix the intercom ...'

20 UNLIKELY THINGS TO READ IN A

'That's the problem, travelling with EasyWardrobe, we've ended up in a small field *miles* from Narnia.'

Winnie the Pooh took all his friends to Spain, where Eeyore was chucked off the top of the bell tower.

Despite protesting, Mr Tickle was put on the Register.

'Sorry, Big Ears,' said Noddy. 'You have to move out. Meet my new friend, Big Tits.'

'You know what?' said the hungry caterpillar. 'This gastric band has changed my whole lifestyle.'

'See Spot run! Oh, he's made a false start and been disqualified.'

The tiger who came to tea had eaten all the packets in the cupboard, all the food cooking on the stove, all of Daddy's beer, and then he ripped Sophie's head off and ate that.

And the caterpillar ate one apple, two pears, a pickle, a piece of salami, a cup cake, developed a wheat intolerance and never became a butterfly.

'I'm sorry, Charlie,' said Willy Wonka. 'I can't give you the factory, I'm laying off all the Oompa Loompas; I've accepted a takeover bid from Kraft.'

'I do not like green eggs and ham,' said the Health and Safety inspector.

'I feel strangely calm today,' said Mr Prozac.

James was very disappointed to discover it wasn't actually a giant peach and that he was, in fact, a midget.

He has knobbly knees and turned-out toes,
And a poisonous wart at the end of his nose,
His eyes are orange, his tongue is black,
He has purple prickles all over his back,
Oh help, oh no, it's Charlie Sheen!

'Did you hear about Badger, Ratty? He's been gassed to halt the spread of TB.'

'Bad news, Noddy, it's actually Parkinson's.'

As Mr Moonface climbed down the magic Faraway tree, he saw Pete Doherty lying face down in the grass.

'Today Hogwarts is closed due to industrial action.'

Just as Mrs Brown was about to usher Paddington into the taxi, he was taken by Russians, who made him dance on a hotplate at their circus.

'These bacon sandwiches taste delicious,' said Winnie the Pooh. 'Don't they, Piglet. Piglet?'

22 *BAD THINGS TO HEAR AT YOUR*

'By the way, you're adopted.'

'Quick! The rest of the family are here. Get back in the cellar!'

'Oh yeah, Harry, you're a wizard but don't worry, you haven't missed out on anything, and I'm sure you'll have a great career at Argos.'

'Me and your mum clubbed together and bought you a prostitute.'

'We've bought you a big bucket of Clearasil.'

'OK, turn the music down now, time for Scrabble.'

'Hello Tracey, I'm the Justin Bieber fan you've been talking to online. I'm Barry, a fifty-two-year-old truck driver.'

'We were going to invite all your friends and have a surprise party, but we thought what you'd really love is to come and watch *Mamma Mia* with me and your mum.'

'Your dad was really James Hewitt.'

'Ladies and gentlemen, please raise your glasses and drink a toast to the Prime Minister.'

'Any of Sebastian's friends for a tumbler of squash?'

'Sixteen? That means you're legal now. Come and sit on your Uncle Bert's knee.'

'We've put some really funny pictures of you up on Facebook.'

'Oh look, it's a card from Manchester United. Isn't that nice. They're saying you've been transferred to Accrington Stanley.'

'Right, you're on your own now. There's the door.'

'Sit down in the lounge, the clown's coming to do some tricks.'

'The time has come to explain to you about what happens when a lady and a man want to make a baby, but instead of talking about it your mum and me are going to demonstrate.'

'Happy birthday! Now let's give thanks to Jesus.'

'You've failed all your GCSEs except needlework, Steve.'

'Right, you're old enough now. Here's your brush. Get up the chimney.'

24 UNLIKELY GREETINGS CARDS

Sorry To Hear You're Leaving And Sorry I Couldn't Find A Better Way To Sack You Than This Card

I Know Where You Live

Congratulations On Your Acquittal Due To A Technicality

Sorry To Hear About Your Mother. On The Plus Side, You Can Afford That New House Now

Sorry To See Your Sex Tape Has Been Leaked On The Internet

I Can't Believe You're 40! (You Look Like Shit)

Have A Wonderful Final Three Weeks Of Life

Happy Diamond Jubilee Your Majesty, From All Your Loyal Subjects. There You Go, That's Saved Millions Of Pounds

Congratulations On Becoming Ambassador To Syria

Roses Are Red, Ivy Is Green, You Showed Me Your Tits, Here Is My Spleen

26 UNLIKELY HEALTH INSURANCE

What's up with you, then? ....

How long's your cock? If you do not have a cock, please skip to the next question. ....

How big are your tits? ....

Do you suffer from any of the following: open sores, buboes, armies of ants coming out of your pores, an alien coming out of your stomach, fat ankles? ☐ YES ☐ NO

Have you, in the last year, lain down with a man? ☐ YES ☐ NO

Do you have heavy buttocks? Sagging breasts? ☐ YES ☐ NO

When did you last cry, you big, soft bastard?

Do you suffer from vertigo, impetigo, indigo or calico?

Any traces of blood in your stools? If not, how about any other items of furniture? ....

Do my fingers smell? What of? ....

Do you have any problems 'down below', if you know what I mean?

If you are male, please skip to the end. If you're a lady, please give us as much information as you can, ooh yeah, that's good, don't stop …

Are you gay? If so, skip or mince to the next question.

Do you suffer fools gladly?

Have you visited your doctor in the last five years? How is he?

How often do you exercise, Fatty?

How long have you been at your current address? If you are a mayfly, please skip to the end.

Do you ever masturbate using your left hand? If not, you should try it – it feels like someone else doing it for you.

Do you find farts funny?   ☐ YES   ☐ NO

Do you find ticking boxes stressful? If yes, tick this box.   ☐

Does it hurt when you pee? What's the longest piss you've ever done? Have you ever done a shit so big it wouldn't flush?

Are you covered in boils? Ugh!

ENTRIES FROM A USELESS DIARY

HOLIDAYS & FESTIVALS

31st January Arsenal Last-Minute Panic Buying Day	**3rd February** National Poo Week Begins	**7th March** Fictitious Family Member Funeral
10th April *Trevor Eve*	**11th May** Likeliest First Day When All The Girls Are Dressing Skimpily	**15th June** Ray Stubbs's Birthday
16th July Satanic Feast Day of *Shabiri – Demon of Blindness*	**31st August** Arsenal Last-Minute Panic Buying Day	**22nd September** Retail Christmas begins
26th October Mysterious Religious Holiday You Can Take Whatever Your Faith	**29th November** Public Holiday In Burkina Faso	**31st December** The End Of The World (Again)

MEASURES & CONVERSIONS

Cwt: Measurement that looks a bit rude at a glance

US Paper Sizes: (This is really important)

1 foot: Heather Mills's nickname

10 pints: Just getting warmed up, yer big ponce

1 Euro: Sod all, unless you're German

Hectare: Posh way of saying 'Hector'

Useful numbers: National Rail Enquiries,
Heathrow Airport,
Buxom Barbara, 22 and new in town

Ton: 1.015 Eric Pickleses

1 ounce: Depends where you get it, man; I paid
£100 to Kelvin in West Ken for some
seriously good shit

12 inches: 1 penis (for any normal man, anyway)

30 BAD THINGS TO HEAR AT YOUR

'By the way, you're adopted.'

'The kids are crying upstairs, something about shitting the bed ...'

'Well that's basically most of your life gone. You will probably never achieve any of your dreams now.'

'Since you're obviously too old to have kids now, shall we get married?'

'Who wants to go clubbing?'

'Everyone join hands and praise Jesus.'

'Police! We've had a tip-off there may be drugs on the premises.'

'Since you're 40, you should probably have a prostate check. Shall we do it now?'

'You're pregnant!'

'No man in this family has lived past forty-one.'

'Charles, I think I'm going to be Queen until I'm a hundred.'

'I've got the results of your prostate check. Shall I read them out?'

'The police are here, they want to know your whereabouts on 16 June 1991 and a DNA sample.'

'Haven't seen you for years. Wait a minute, what's that on your face? It looks malignant.'

'Wow! I would never have guessed! You look amazing for your age! Oh sorry, you said you're forty? Oh . . OK.'

'I loved being forty, best year of my life. I was forty-one when it all went wrong; I went bald, got really fat and ended up with this colostomy bag ...'

'Life begins at forty, eh? That's a load of bollocks, innit?'

'We've all clubbed together and bought you a Thai bride; here he is.'

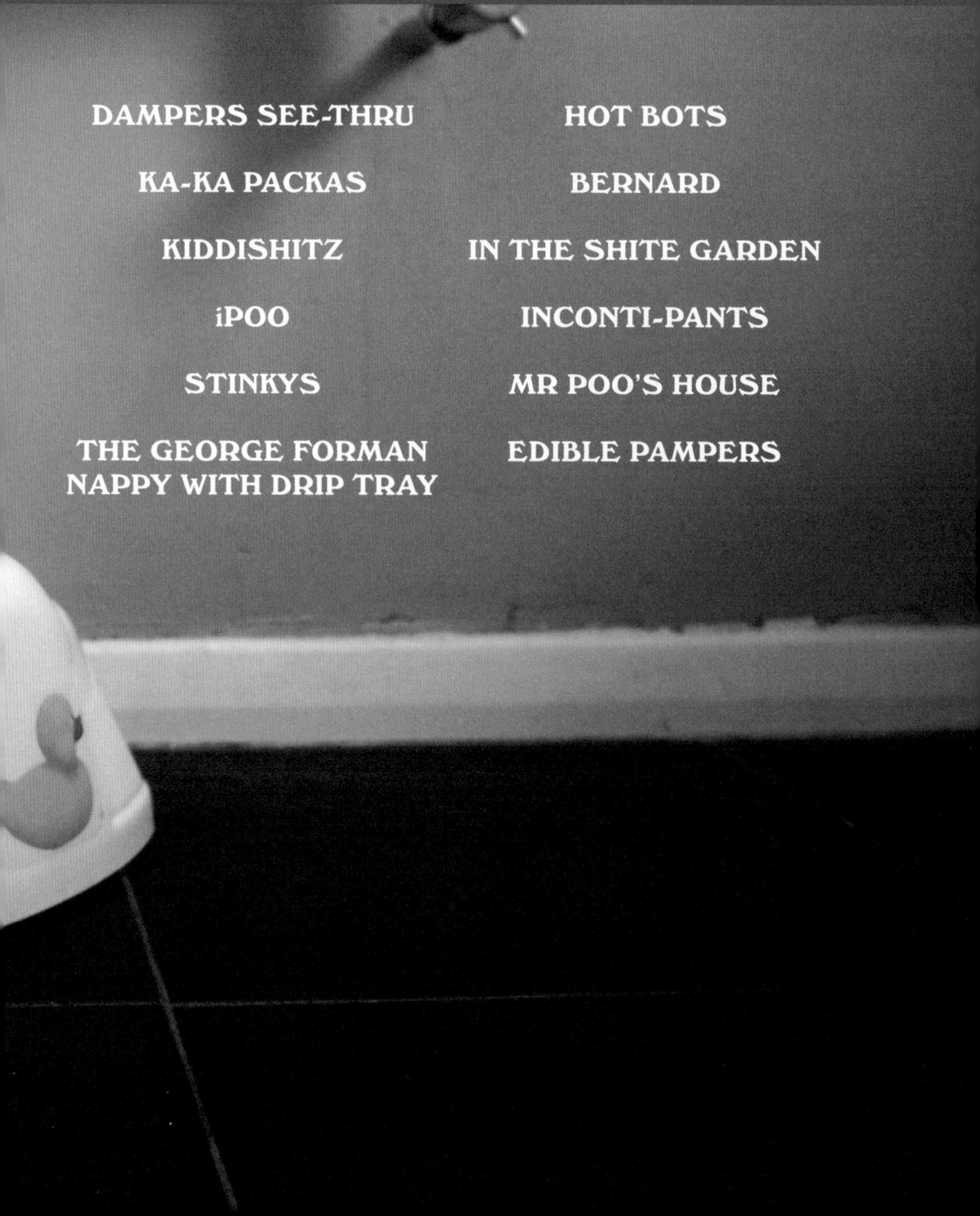

DAMPERS SEE-THRU

KA-KA PACKAS

KIDDISHITZ

iPOO

STINKYS

THE GEORGE FORMAN
NAPPY WITH DRIP TRAY

HOT BOTS

BERNARD

IN THE SHITE GARDEN

INCONTI-PANTS

MR POO'S HOUSE

EDIBLE PAMPERS

1. **Rampant Peter Rabbit**

2. **My Little Gypsy**

3. **Teenage Mutants**

4. **Somali Pirate Ship**

5. **Landmine Twister!**

6. **My First Sex-Worker Dolly** Comes with five recorded phrases! Pull the string and watch her go!
'Me so horny!'
'No kissing!'
'Would you like to buy me a drink?'
'What do you want my name to be?'
'I'm doing this to fund my degree!'

7. **Klaus Barbie**

8. **My Little Goebbels**

9. **Nico-Patch Dolls**

10. **Hungry Hippos** (Actual Size)

11. **Mouse Crap**

12. **Loose Women Lego**

13. **Connect 2**

14. **Ker-Spunk!**

15. Paedo!

16. My First Lead Bear

17. My Little Mimsy

18. Electrified Slinky

19. Pin the Cock on the Donkey

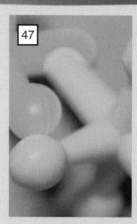

47

20. Racist Action Figure Comes with six recorded phrases! Pull the string and watch him go!
'If you don't like it here, go home!'
'More poppadoms over here, Genghis!'
'I'm not racist but …'
'We're just a small country!'
'They're takin' our jobs!'

81

21. Bi-Polar Pit Bull

22. Mrs Slocombe's Pussy

23. Slippy the Asphyxiating Snake

24. Mr Rooney Head – Attach funny new hair and ears!

39

25. Happy Slap!

26. NHS Operation – Open the box and do the paperwork! Assess budgets! And loads more fun!

27. A Nuclear Physics Set

36 UNLIKELY LETTERS TO AN AGONY

Dear Agony Aunt ...

I was photographed sunbathing topless in the papers, now my colleagues at work are laughing at me because they've seen my breasts. Please help, Brian from Newcastle.

• • • • • • • • • • • • • • • • •

Dear Agony Aunt, my lover is a wild animal in bed, and the government says the circus has to get rid of him.

• • • • • • • • • • • • • • • • •

I have curvature of the penis. There's a clinic round the corner that can help – but I'm worried they might see me coming.

Dear Deidre, I have a serious problem with my husband of ten years. Could you please trivialize it by turning it into a photostory starring much younger models in their pants?

• • • • • • • • • • • • • • • • •

I am a ninety-year-old man, and I am having trouble getting an erection. Especially since I am trying to get one by looking at a ninety-year-old woman.

• • • • • • • • • • • • • • • • •

Please help, I can't stop masturbating. I seem to be doing it all the time. P.S. Please excuse the shaky handwriting.

• • • • • • • • • • • • • • • • •

My wife said I could have anal sex for my birthday, now she won't talk to me or the bloke I had it with.

★ ★

AUNT

Please help, I'm a sex addict – can you come and give me a right good banging?

Am I wrong to fancy my teacher, especially as it's my mum who's just in to help out for the day?

My husband insists on having anal sex when it's my birthday. Trouble is, I have a real birthday and an official birthday.

I am 26 and my girlfriend is 36. Is ten years too great an age gap in a relationship? I need to know, because she's got a cracking 16-year-old daughter.

All my girlfriend does all day is moan, moan, moan. She's a female tennis player and she's starting to get on my nerves.

My wife is a journalist currently writing a weekly Agony Aunt column. While she's out working, I am banging her sister …

Dear Deirdre, I've just had sex with my wife's sister. I don't want any advice, I just want to brag about it.

Dear Agony Aunt, can I ask what happened to your Agony Uncle, or don't you like to talk about it?

My new wife insists on being treated like a princess. What am I to do? Yours, Mike Tindall.

Can you help? I'm an old man of 85 and many years ago I wrote a book about fly fishing …

38 *UNLIKELY THINGS TO HEAR ON A*

'So my best suggestion for how you can look good naked – turn out the light.'

'Dear God, are you the "after"?'

'Following the success of *Snog Marry Avoid*, BBC3 present their new show – *Stalk Rape Murder*.'

'Wow, your mum really does look ten years younger – that's the best embalming I've ever seen.'

'Our challenge was to get Paul McCartney looking younger for his wedding. We failed.'

'Great – you've applied the seventh layer of make-up to your face. Now you're ready to take to the skies and pour coffee over the passengers' laps.'

'First wait till it's dark and then hide up a tree outside their bedroom window with a pair of binoculars. You're watching *How to Get A Good Look At Someone Naked*.'

'With a pair of Spanx to hold in the tummy and a good supporting bra to stop the breasts sagging, Trevor looks great.'

'After putting her lipstick on, she now looks like an oil painting. Unfortunately it's a Picasso.'

'Listen girlfriend, no one will bat an eyelid when I put you in the shop window naked – it's a butchers'.'

'Here's what we'll do – we'll get you a professional make-up artist, an expert hairdresser, some expensive clothes and then photograph you cleverly using studio lighting from the most flattering angles. And hey presto, you look a bit better. It's a simple as that.'

'To improve your looks I suggest you wear a big pair of fat controlling pants, over your face.'

'After two hours with the eyebrow tweezers, you'd never know Edna once had a moustache.'

'I really think it'll spoil the effect of looking good naked if you insist on keeping your socks on.'

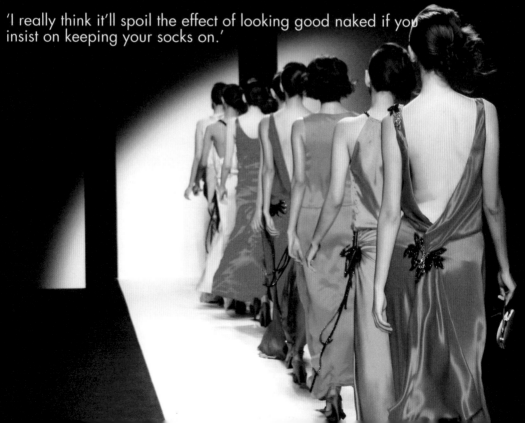

40 *UNLIKELY THINGS TO READ ON A*

Here lies Alexander Litvinenko. Hazchem. Danger! Authorized Personnel Only.

Run! It *was* catching!!

Gone to meet 'the man upstairs', he said. Sadly, that man was an escaped serial killer.

Unexpectedly taken from us, 7 June 1998 – after his arrest, he died in police custody.

He never married … (nudge, nudge)

Willie Jones, 1827–2009. Grandfather, father, husband, sister, priest, air-sea rescue pilot, compulsive liar.

Here lies Christopher J. Jones, 1620–1650. Shame he only lived half an hour.

I know, I thought he'd died years ago too.

We got him.

Lord preserve him as he was when he went. Only without the fishnets and the orange in his mouth.

Here lies Arthur Stevens, the world's most evil lift attendant. Going down?

HIS FINAL WORDS
REALLY DO SAY IT
ALL:

"ARRGH!
MY CHEST! CALL A
FUCKING AMB——"

42 UNLIKELY THINGS TO READ ON

This site has closed down unexpectedly, as your wife is walking up the stairs.

You look like you're about write a letter! Are you living in the 1930s? Write an email. Twat.

Please click here to pretend you have read the terms and conditions.

Buffering is in progress ... to be honest, you might as well go and make your dinner.

I'm a Nigerian prince and I'm more than happy with the amount of money I have.

A sad and lonely person, who vaguely knows you, wants to be your friend on Facebook.

Banging the mouse on the desk will not make me work any quicker.

Welcome to your Myspace log in page.

Welcome to the website that's all about processed pork and ham luncheon meat. Would you like us to send you regular emails abut our products?

Welcome to Wikileaks – by the time this page refreshes, a US rendition team will be beating the shit out of you.

44 UNLIKELY NEWSPAPER BIRTH

OUR LITTLE BUNDLE just couldn't wait, she arrived 4 weeks ahead of her date! Still, it's given us more time to sort out the adoption papers.

TRIPLETS! ARRGH! Anyone want one? Will sell to a good home.

A SON: *Rio Rooney Fergie*. Let's hope he doesn't grow up wanting to support City.

9 LBS 8 OZ Jennifer arrived yesterday after a long and painful birth. Here's a link to the YouTube video; it get's really horrid at about 08.02.

TEN LITTLE FINGERS, TEN LITTLE TOES, but unfortunately two quite big heads and no genitalia.

WE'VE HAD A BABY! A new life beginning just as ours is fucking ending. Farewell everyone we used to have a nice time with down the pub.

IT'S A BOY!
(We think – it's bloody ugly.)

TREBLE THE LOVE and treble the joy! Now we're fucked: two girls and a boy!

MY LOVELY WUBBLY WIFE and I are celebrating the emergence of a tiny ickle babba from her front bottom. We've called him Tyson.

A GIRL! And if anyone thinks of laying a finger on my princess, I'll kill 'em.

DAVID AND VICTORIA BECKHAM are delighted to announce the birth of their fifth child. Working title: 'Project V'.

A BOY! Named Sue! That should make his life easy.

NEWS FROM KEITH: a beautiful baby boy! Like the previous one but with a much fitter mum.

A NEW LITTLE PERSON HAS ARRIVED! Check out his tour dates at jamiecullum.com

A BEAUTIFUL BABY GIRL. Mother delighted. Father(s) anxiously waiting on a phone call from a researcher on *The Jeremy Kyle Show*.

A BABY is cuddles and tickles on toes, the sweet scent of powder and shit up your nose.

PEREGRINE ALGERNON WILBERFORCE TODGER, born 16 April, London. Good luck at school, mate.

The stork has come by and it was no surprise, it left us ... Horribly traumatized as it thrashed around frenziedly in our baby's bedroom.

MATTHEW is 21 inches long, 7 lbs 11 oz, which coincidentally are the exact dimensions of the father's penis.

46 UNLIKELY THINGS TO HEAR ON A

'And now the news in the shitty place that you live.'

'Next, why police cuts mean no sirens for patrol cars. Here's Nina Nana.'

'An enhanced fiscal policy on the Eurozone was today ... Oh, I don't know what I'm talking about.'

'Now over to a slightly frightening head-girl type for the sport.'

'Now for more news on Wayne Rooney's latest hat-trick – if he puts it on and off quickly enough, you can't tell he's had a transplant.'

'Here are the headlines. Britain has been caught in a time warp and thrown back thirty years. I'm Selina Scott.'

'And now for the weather forecast, let's hope it's a hot one. Oh no, it's Rob McElwee.'

'Our reporter is live in Libya, which is annoying as all of the action is in Syria.'

'In line with BBC policy, in the following interview Sir Alex Ferguson's words will be read out by an actor.'

'And do send us your ill-informed bigoted views.'

'Nick, that George Osborne's a c**t isn't he?'

'And now the dull Welsh story that we put in to keep Huw Edwards happy.'

'And now the news where you are: your dinner's late and your wife's got the hump.'

'And next, our report on healthy eating. Viewers in Scotland have their own programme.'

'For the latest on the nuclear crisis, press the red button – not you, Prime Minister!'

'Hello and welcome to *BBC Breakfast* where for the thirty-second duration of this shot, I can say anything I like because you're all too busy looking up Susanna Reid's skirt.'

'So, who should prevail, Ed Balls or Ed Miliband? Well, let's ask our Economics Editor, Stephanie Flanders, who has been porked by both.'

'And now a news story based in Italy, giving Fiona Bruce the chance to do a ridiculous Dolmio-man accent every time she reads out a name.'

'And now with the day's sport, one of our slightly less-good

48 *UNLIKELY THINGS FOR A TEACHER*

'I'd like you to demonstrate how to put on a condom using, errm … my cock.'

'Right, blacks on one side, whites on the other.'

'Hello, I'm the new supply teacher, so go easy on me! My name is Gerald Ballsucker.'

'Before we go, let's pray to our lord, mighty Satan.'

'You're all invited to a party at my parents' house tonight.'

'So all you need is some fertilizer, some nails, a rucksack …'

'You really remind me of my wife, Simpkins.'

'Clothes are so restrictive.'

'Pete, I know you're only five, but your drawing of your mum totally lacked light and shade; it was one big artistic cliché.'

'OK, we are going to be doing a chemical practical. This is LSD …'

'I've got a gun and I'm not afraid to use it.'

'Penelope, great essay – and even better tits!'

'We're not doing the Nativity, we're going to do the Passion of the Christ.'

'We are going to do role play, who wants to be a customs inspector?'

'Let's do hymn number forty-three ... "Deutschland, Deutschland".'

'Before the school trip let me remind you class, what happens on tour, stays on tour.'

'This is an exercise in trust: now put the apple on your head.'

'A jolly good morning to you, boys. Now let's get down to some wicked learnin' in dis hood.'

'The theme for tomorrow's assembly is St Trinian's.'

'I'm just a man, standing before a class, trying to get them to love him ...'

'Don't be shy now, who wants to sit on my lap?'

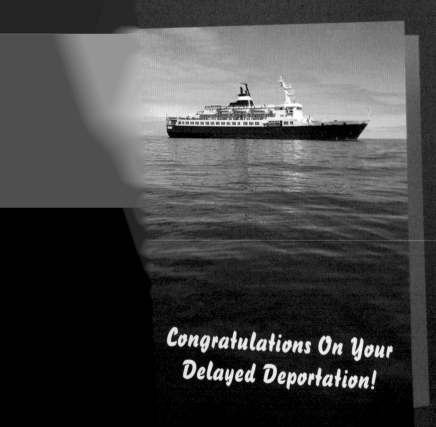

Congratulations On Your
Delayed Deportation!

Happy 100th Birthday. Have A Great Day (Even Though You Won't Have A Fucking Clue What's Going On)

Roses Are Red, So Don't Be Glum, My Wife's Away, Fancy One Up The Bum?

With Deepest Sympathy And Stuff

To My Wife On Our Silver Wedding Anniversary, Here Are Our Divorce Papers

Hello. I'd Like To Be Your Friend? Confirm?

You've Come Out! Ooh Get Her!

To A Wonderful Mummy, Could You Please Remove This Curse From My Family?

You've Had A Boy! (Best Keep It Quiet, Though. He Only 'Said' He Was 16)

Happy 70th Birthday, Sir Alex Ferguson (Though Going Off Your Measurement Of Time It Should Be Happy 105th)

Roses Are Green, Violets Are Pink, Looks Like I've Overdone The Medication Again

52 *UNLIKELY THINGS TO READ IN A*

Divide it up yourselves, you money-grabbing bastards!

I would like my ashes to be spread at the place where I spent my happiest times ... in the pants of my wife's sister.

You can have the money if you sit in a bath of baked beans for 34 days.

In the event of my death, I would like my title to miss my son Charles and pass to my grandson William as it would be fucking hilarious.

And the main beneficiary is ... (long *X Factor*-style pause)

OK, Doreen, you've got the car, now you can gamble that and go for the house and land by answering this question ...

The bulk of my £20 million fortune will be left to General Abuja of Nigeria, who approached me with a wonderful scheme that should set up my family for life.

In the event of me dying before my wife, I want her closely questioned by the police.

In order to ease the family's inheritance-tax burden, I have resolved to leave them fuck all.

To my wife and children I leave my Bay City Rollers albums and the 1977 *Magpie* annual.

In the event of my death, I would like to have my penis cryogenically frozen and reanimated at such a time when science has advanced sufficiently.

To my loving wife Judith, I leave £7.35.

In the event of my death, I would really like to be jettisoned into the sea by the US military. Cheers, Osama bin Laden.

After my death, I would like to be cremated and played for by the cricket teams of England and Australia.

To my beloved cat Tufty, I leave £20 million on the condition he never marries and the money must be held in a trust until he is 21.

I would like to divide my fortune between my three wives in the hope the money will soften the blow of their finding out about each other.

I'd like to erect a memorial at the place where I met the love of my life: a public toilet on Hampstead Heath.

My children assured me all they really wanted were the fun memories of our time together, so I've given their £12 million to the Tory Party.

In the event of my extraordinary wooden-leg-related accidental death, I hereby bequeath my sizeable fortune to my dear wife, Heather Mills.

To my son, I leave my 3.6 million Twitter followers. Ha! LOL! #Thatsallhesgetting

I, an eccentric, reclusive billionaire, whom nobody in my family has ever met, resolve to leave all the money to my next of kin with no weird conditions.

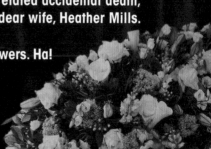

54 UNLIKELY ETIQUETTE TIPS

Remember: lavatory, never toilet. Sofa, never settee. Supper, never tea. Front bottom, never minge.

In the event of being on the receiving end of an unfortunate faux pas, try to brush it off with a tinkling laugh, followed by a knee to the groin and swift use of a broken glass to the face.

When nature calls, excuse yourself from the group. Leave it clean, always flush and never discuss – unless it was an absolute monster.

If stuck for a conversational topic, weather never falters, but as a plan B, "immigrants" is usually quite a banker.

Unless in a very informal setting, don't dunk anything in your tea – especially your genitals.

Talk to every woman as if you loved her, every man as if he loved you, and you should get your end away most nights.

In rural Britain it is still the norm to say a friendly hello to people you may encounter, although if you are clearly foreign or of ethnic origin, don't expect a reply.

Don't make mobile calls from inappropriate locations: a bathroom conversation is off-putting, though if you are having a shit and are between strains they'll probably never know.

When meeting in-laws for the first time never get more drunk than them unless they're really boring teetotal bastards.

Be tolerant if sudden lurches on public transport propel you into close proximity with another passenger, but obviously don't pass up the opportunity for a subtle grope.

A sincere apology should always be offered when your actions have impacted negatively on another person, unless they're c**ts.

Think about what your ringtone choice will say about you and take the opportunity of a train journey to sit and go through every option on your phone.

When you don't know people well, it is advisable not to talk about death, disease, religion and anal sex.

Always pass the port to the left and never ask for it to change direction. This is a criminal offence in Britain and carries a maximum sentence of 30 years.

Overuse of foreign phrases in English conversation can seem rather *outré*, *passé* and somewhat *fin de siècle*.

There is little etiquette to the writing of postcards as this is only done by quite dreadful working-class people.

When having guests to stay, don't be a martyr. Feel free to suggest to your guest that they should fuck off and die.

If you are sharing a bedroom with your partner at your in-laws, be discreet. Try gagging her or putting your fist in her mouth during sex to muffle any noise.

When leaving the toilet after a call of nature, it is polite to say, 'I'd give that a couple of minutes', if you have performed a number two ablution.

Women should wear a hat to Royal Ascot and smart race meetings as they are perfect for storing fags under or covering your arse crack when you bend over.

Treat a troublesome in-law like you would childhood chicken pox: constantly moan about them, pray they'll soon go and repeatedly scratch them.

When new neighbours move in, pop round with a friendly smile, a cup of tea and a spycam to install in the bedroom mirror.

56 BAD THINGS TO HEAR IN A

'What happens in the "Big Room" behind those metal doors?'

'Run for your lives!'

'Hello, Mrs Jones. Don't be alarmed but this is a priest and your next of kin.'

'OK, everybody up. Those rocks won't break themselves.'

'They're sex mad in here.'

'Welcome to the first meeting of the escape committee.'

'Everyone get tooled up. There's some bluds from the Laurel Vale massive outside on mobility scooters.'

'When Andy Dufresne walked into the Shawshank Residential Care Home, I knew he wasn't your average inmate.'

'Will everyone convene in the Sun Lounge for the foam party and Miss Wet T-Shirt competition.'

'Hello. I'll just rest my scythe against the door.'

'It is now Happy Hour at the Horlicks Bar.'

'First rule of Fight Club. You do not talk about Fight Club.'

'Residents are reminded that the gun amnesty stays in place until January 22nd.'

'Can I have a happy finish with my bed bath, please?'

'Hello, Room Service? I'd like a bottle of the Petrus and two glasses, the stroganoff and the lamb up to room 362.'

'Morning, everyone. It's time for your bleep test.'

'Shall I change the sheets or is this a dirty protest?'

'Nurse, I'm just having trouble opening this ZIP file on my email. Could you help me?'

58 *UNLIKELY THINGS TO HEAR ON A*

'With so much cupboard space and a loft above, the opportunities for voyeurism in the bedroom are enormous.'

'Instantly you can see how much roomier it is once we've taken out the old lady and her oxygen cylinders.'

'Well, I don't know whether these viewers are serious buyers or not, but as soon as they've finished taking a dump we'll ask them.'

'So you snapped it up at auction for £100,000. What exactly do you plan to do with Middlesbrough?'

'So through here you've converted two rooms into one. And that's created one good-size room, with a ridiculously high ceiling.'

'They've solved the problem of parking, but not having a lounge might devalue the property.'

'Coincidentally, this house, which once belonged to Anne Robinson, has been sandblasted so much it's unrecognizable.'

'The rear garden is south-facing. As indeed is the front garden. On the downside it can be quite chilly here at the North Pole.'

'Mr Jobson was nagged by his wife to do all the DIY himself, which he did, including this wonderful patio, which he laid shortly after she disappeared.'

'At the moment the land is a barren, inhospitable wasteland. But the owners have an ambitious plan to stage a World Cup here.'

'Remember, the value of your property can go down as well as plummet.'

'I'm Phil and this is Kirsty, welcome to Repossession, Repossession, Repossession.'

'Well, we brought the estate agents round to value the property, and taking into account all your work on it, they've said two-seven-five, two-eight-five, maybe even as high as three pounds.'

'Well, that is unusual, you've knocked your kitchen into … the neighbour's kitchen. They will be surprised.'

'And in this delightful corner of Greece you are actually within an easy walk of one of Europe's oldest nuclear reactors.'

'This week on *Home or Away*, Mr Henderson is choosing between a villa in Spain or a house in Doncaster. Well, it's a villa in Spain, isn't it? See you next week.'

'The wonderful thing about *Grand Designs* is that every week I think I can't hate the people on it any more, and every week I can.'

'The Joneses are looking for a house near a really good school. Because Mr Jones is a paedophile.'

'Kirstie and I agreed to meet Ben and Emma at the house when the vendors were away, hoping that the combination of a lovely sunny day and the chance to relax a bit might persuade them to join us naked in the hot tub.'

'This is one of the most sought-after houses … in Sunderland.'

'Kevin and Michelle are looking to buy a villa in Southern Spain. They've got a budget of six million pounds in gold bullion from Kevin's last job, the NatWest, Walthamstow. And they want to move in tonight.'

'This flat in Brixton is worth two hundred thousand – but the contents of the greenhouse and the loft are worth an awful lot more.'

60 UNLIKELY THINGS TO HEAR ON A

'Slow down, position yourself parallel to the kerb while I pick out a prostitute.'

'I'm going to have to fail you, Mr Michael, so if you'd like to reverse out of Snappy Snaps …'

'Take the wheel while I wind down the window … PIGS!'

'Hello? Oh Mum, it's you, I'm on my driving test … No, it's not going well.'

'When I tap the windscreen, let's see if the bloke in the car wakes up.'

'You did fine on the driving but you failed by not shouting enough abuse at other road users.'

'Let's say if the cyclist lives, I'll pass you.'

'Congratulations, you've passed. You now get to spend ten grand a year on insurance.'

'I've always found a stiff Scotch helps me relax before driving tests.'

'OK, Mr Starsky, I'd like you to do a handbrake turn into that pile of empty cardboard boxes.'

'OK, let's practise the emergency stop, I'm dying for a piss.'

'I'm just nibbling your ear, don't let it distract you.'

'Continue driving for twenty-five minutes, and when I tap the dashboard, stop and let me out because I'll be home.'

'Right, can you reverse around this corner on two wheels?' 'Don't worry, we can lose them on this estate.'

'Could you possibly try going the right way up the M4?'

'When I said wait until I hit the dashboard, I didn't mean with my face.'

'Right, can you see those twelve people lying down in a row and the big ramp?'

'Speed camera. So slow down and then accelerate away again.'

'Let's set it to hyperdrive.'

'I won't bother indicating, everyone knows I live down this road.'

'Do you mind if I pick a few mates up and crank up the stereo?'

'I don't know where the indicators are – I only stole it this morning.'

'OK, you weren't too good on your three-point turn but let's see how you are at "jumping the ravine".'

62 UNLIKELY SCHOOL REPORT

TEACHERS' REMARKS

Dear Mr and Mrs Harris, young Rolf is annoying the shit out of everyone.

Dear Mr and Mrs Huhne, Chris is a lovely boy but he really needs to slow down.

Dear Mr and Mrs Radcliffe, Paula is a talented girl but she must remember school rules: no running or shitting in the corridor.

Dear Mr and Mrs Clegg, Nick has gone into his shell somewhat this term after becoming friendly with the Cameron boy.

Dear Mr and Mrs Pan, Peter shows tremendous promise, but he really needs to grow up.

DEAR MR RAMSDEN, HARRY REALLY IS A CHIP OFF THE OLD BLOCK, BUT HE COULD DO BATTER.

Dear Mrs and Mrs Wenger, Arsène is doing wonderfully in French, but I'm sorry to tell you that he has yet again failed his eye test.

Dear Mr and Mrs Milliband, David has been a bit upset by Ed standing against him as milk monitor.

TEACHERS' REMARKS

Dear Mr and Mrs Gascoigne, Paul has had a few problems this year but as I've told him, as long as he keeps hold of his chicken and his fishing rod, he'll be fine.

DEAR MR AND MRS MOSLEY, I'VE BEEN VERY IMPRESSED WITH HOW WELL MAX RESPONDS TO DISCIPLINE.

DEAR MR AND MRS AHMADINEJAD, MAHMOUD CONTINUES TO EXCEL IN PHYSICS BUT HE MUST BE MORE WILLING TO SHOW HIS WORK.

Dear Mr and Mrs Bush, George is continuing to find academic work difficult and lags behind most of his class, but I suppose not everyone will grow up to be the President, will they!

Dear Mr and Mrs Qatada, Abu has been very badly behaved this term and we'd really like to punish him further but unfortunately we can't.

Dear Mr and Mrs Prescott, we continue to be amazed by what a gifted natural athlete John is. A future Olympian, perhaps?

64 UNLIKELY BOOK TITLES

Dicken About by Charles Dickens

Marr and Par: Andrew Marr's Making of Modern Golf

I Have a Dream by John Terry

Alliss in Wonderland: The Collected LSD-fuelled Musings of Peter Alliss

Who the Fuck is Alliss? The Secret Diaries of Sandy Lyle

Oliver's Twist: Jamie Oliver's Guide to Pontoon

A Knight to Forget: The biography of Fred Goodwin

Harry Redknapp's Guide to Self-Assessment Tax

The Joy of Sketchley's

Flanders and Swann: England Offspinner Graham Swann Explores World War I Battlefields

The Forsyth Saga: The Selected Letters of Sir Bruce Forsyth

Alliss Doesn't Live Here Any More:

The Memoirs of the Bloke Who Bought Peter Alliss's Surrey Bungalow in 1987

66 UNLIKELY FOOTBALL CHANTS

'You're Going To Get Your Fucking Head Massaged'

'You're Shit And I'm Not Sure You're Aware Of That (So I Thought It Was Worth Pointing Out)'

'3-0! And Really It's Against The Run of Play'

'Heskey's Scored, Heskey's Scored, Heskey's Scored'

'Ad Augusta Per Angusta! Ad Augusta Per Angusta!'

'Walking Off. Refusing To Move. Sulking In A Tevez Wonderland'

'Manchester La La La. If United Don't Win, I'd Like It To Be City'

'Going Down, Going Down, Going Down, Is What Your Wife's Doing To Ryan Giggs'

'One Humphrey Twistleton-Wickham, There's Only One Humphrey Twistleton-Wickham'

'It's Not Like Watching Brazil At All, Really'

'Who's The Bitch In The Black?'

'Get Your Cock Out For The Lads'

'He's John Terry, He Parks Where He Likes'

'Who Ate All The Filet Mignons?'

'Fergie, Fergie, What's The Score? I Haven't Been Watching'

'Statistically, One Of Your Players Could Well Be Gay'

'Millwall! Millwall! Rah Rah Rah!'

'Green Shorts With Orange Shirts? You're Having A Laugh'

'Stand Up If You Love Jesus, Stand Up If You Love Jesus'

'You're Fairly Limited As A Footballer! Ahhhhhhhh!'

'Let's All Do The Charleston'

'He's Small, He's Quick, He's Linguistically Naïve When It Comes To Terms Of Racial Identity, Suár-ez, Suár-ez'

68 *UNLIKELY NAMES FOR NEWBORNS*

TWO DOGS FUCKING

FANNY

RUMPELSTILTSKIN

KUNDT

ROSACEA

FINDUS CRISPY PANCAKE

JUDAS

NORBIT

SAVLON

THREE DOGS FUCKING

ONE DOG WANKING

RUSTY BEDSPRING

HUGO FUKURSELF

STUBBSY

BEELZEBUB

70 *UNLIKELY THINGS TO HEAR ON A*

'Having booked the easyJet flight to Benidorm, Mr Jones was very disappointed when he got there – it was a real shithole.'

'This week on *Watchdog*, the scandalous rip-off that means millions of people pay a licence fee, and in return they get shit like this.'

'It's broken, it doesn't work properly and it's not what I ordered – tonight we look at the coalition.'

'Tonight we investigate the decorators who painted the town red in this week's *Rouge Traders.*'

'Dear *Watchdog*, having purchased tickets for Glastonbury I was appalled to find myself disturbed by the incessant playing of loud music.'

'This plumber charges over six hundred pounds an hour ... unfortunately, not everyone is as cheap as him.'

'Clearly payday loan companies like Wonga.com are not the solution, and Greece will have to find some other way to pay its debts.'

'We also put concealed cameras into the shower room, but we didn't tell our young female researcher about those ones.'

'This week *Watchdog* investigates an outfit that delights in praying on the fears of the elderly – us.'

'Are travellers unfairly stereotyped? We were going to interview them, but didn't want to get our cameras nicked.'

'This week *Watchdog* investigates the TV programme that manages to stretch five minutes of content into an hour.'

'This week we look at a hair dye that makes claims it can't fulfil, which is why I'm still stuck being ginger.'

'This week Anne Robinson looks at bikini-waxing strips – are they one big rip-off?'

'Experts say it's easy to spot which cartons of Pot Noodle have been tampered with, as they taste better.'

'The tar had been badly mixed and there wasn't nearly enough bitumen – this was the worsst motorway service sandwich I'd ever had.'

'This was a clear case of mislabelling, but if putting a size-12 label in a size-16 dress made a fat woman happy, why not?'

'I recently bought a new TV – 56-inch screen with high definition. First face I saw, John McCririck. Who do I sue?'

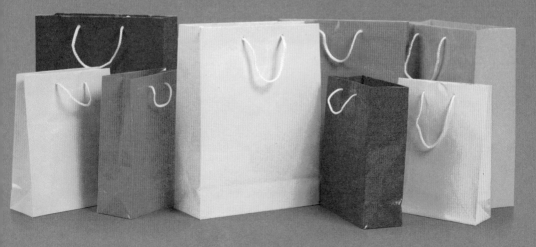

72 UNLIKELY NAMES FOR NAPPY

CRAPPYPANTS

HUGGIES: NOW IN
PRAWN COCKTAIL
FLAVOUR

BIG BOYS

SLOPPIES

HAPPY CRAPPERS

YUCK! WHAT THE FUCK
IS *THAT*?

I CAN'T BELIEVE THESE
AREN'T NAPPIES

DUNG-A-REES

THE NUMBER 2 RANGE

RIBBED FOR THEIR
PLEASURE

74 *UNLIKELY THINGS TO READ ON A*

FELL ASLEEP
ON
AUGUST 16TH 2004.

UNFORTUNATELY

WHILST DRIVING

A TRUCK ON THE

M5

He died doing what he loved: attempting to commit suicide.

Pete Jones, loving father and car mechanic. Died Wednesday 15 June. Though typically he promised us it would be Friday.

May he find happiness when he gets to the other side, unlike the road he was crossing when the taxi hit him.

Here lies the head of MI5 – we don't know where the rest of the body is.

'Accursed be anyone who disturbs these bones.' Dave Stevens, loving husband, father and grandfather 1932–2008.

He loved the ladies and they loved him, so it's only fitting he's entering a large hole in a stiffened state.

Show plot for sale. Jump in, look around and then talk to one of our advisers.

Here lies big Jim Jones. He always wanted to lose weight. He has now.

Here lies the former head of Network Rail, we're sorry that he's late.

Born on a Monday, married on a Tuesday, murdered by Ronnie Kray, turns out he was gay.

Loved social networking. He will be missed. #deadandstuff. God likes this.

Here lies Kim Jong. I told you he was 'il'.

Slow down or you'll never have time to read everything that's written onto this dot-matrix sign – oh, too late

Remember – turn your lights on, if you want people to join you when you're dogging

Pilots – pull up, quick – you're flying too low!

Strictly No U-Turns – unless you're in a coalition government

Welcome To The Midlands – an area of outstanding natural ugliness

Your eyes are heavy, you are feeling sleepy …

Welcome To Middlesbrough – twinned with itself because nowhere else was interested

For Glasgow, take the high road, I'll take the low road and I'll be in Glasgow afore ye

Roadworks until July 2005 – expect delays

Speed kills. So does heroin, smack and ketamine.

Did you leave the gas on?

78 *LINES YOU WOULDN'T HEAR IN A*

'Jenkins, take your trousers down and show M'lady why we call you the "foot" man.'

'Who'd have thought we'd have got together – you, a nurse at the clinic, and me, riddled with the clap.'

'Phwaooar, look at the ankle on that!'

'Oh hang on, that's my mobile.'

'That'll be all for tonight, Hudson, unless you'd like to come upstairs and bum me.'

'A MANbag?!'

'Heathcliff, they say you have a touch of gypsy blood, so for the last time, take that bloody caravan off my field!'

'Mr Darcy, I must declare that you danced a most wonderful Quadrille. Sadly however, Craig Revel Horwood can only give you a five.'

'I told her if she walked through that door it would be the end. But she wouldn't believe the lift was being repaired.'

'She had to choose between two brothers. The handsome, intelligent one, or the ugly geeky one that had the union support.'

'What the fuck is an entail?'

'Bring it in, Jeeves; now, who ordered the lamb bhuna?'

'Farewell Mama, Papa, I shall be going to Glastonbury for the season.'

'For shizzle my nizzle, Lady Bracknell.'

'Last night the debutantes all successfully came out, as indeed did the head footman.'

'Why do you blush so, Elizabeth?'
'Well, it's just that when you came out of the lake I could see your cock.'

'I've been busy in the wine cellar, Sir. I'm now off to polish your shirt and iron your shoes.'

'Hudson, we'll have a light supper tonight – mini kievs and chicken dinosaurs, please.'

'I've drawn your bath for you, Ma'am. It's a rather good likeness – would you like me to get a magnet and attach it to the fridge?'

'Oooh, it's Mr Darcy, be still my beating heart. Argh, my arm's gone numb, arrrgh ...'

80 *UNLIKELY THINGS TO HEAR OVER*

'Clean-up needed in the magazine aisle, between *Loaded* and *Nuts*.'

'The train coming into platform seven has been cancelled, so could the man who has just thrown himself onto the track please go to platform number two, where the express is due any moment.

'British Airways apologize to all passengers travelling to Cardiff. It must be awful for you.'

'The guard will be inspecting tickets during the journey unless there are significant delays in which case he'll be hiding up here with the driver.'

'You are sitting in the quiet carriage, so from now on I'm going to shut the fuck up.'

'Ticket numbers one to fifty, that's one to fifty, Ryan Giggs will shag you now.'

'Ladies and gentlemen, we are just about to draw the raffle for this year's fabulous top prize – an NHS dental appointment.'

'The high-speed train to Birmingham has been delayed for another 100 years thanks to the Tory MPs not wanting it travelling through their gardens.'

'Could Ryanair passengers please not leave baggage unattended. It will be blown up and then you will be charged according to how heavy it was.'

'Could the maintenance engineer please come to the room and fix the ... cracckckkckc zzzzzkkkk.'

'Mr Brian Henderson has got ticket number seventeen. And what a splendid prize that is.'

'Cashier number four is closed. Cashier number two is arguing with an old lady who can't hear properly. Cashier number one has inexplicably vanished for ten minutes. Cashier number six appears to be free but is failing to press her buzzer.'

'Anyone interested in watching a display of old-fashioned bare-knuckle boxing, please make your way to the tea tent, where things have got a bit out of hand.'

'Could Ryanair passengers please proceed to the gate, open the gate, go across the field, over the other gate and ask a man called Steve where the old aerodrome is.'

'Customers looking for our extremely fresh free-range chicken – it has just bolted into the non-food aisle.'

82 UNLIKELY THINGS TO HEAR ON A

'We called British Gas and they assured us that our call was important to them and would be answered shortly.'

'This hair-trigger **TNT** landmine is a potential death trap.'

'Despite the Sale of Goods Act clearly being on their side, Liverpool couldn't get their money back for Andy Carroll.'

'Are you in talks with your bank about a loan? Before you proceed, remember they may not be able to pay you back.'

'Tonight on *Watchdog* we look at the shocking state of TV consumer programmes.'

'If you were sold protection you didn't want, you probably lived in the East End in the 1960s.'

'We investigated Beelzebub Roofing and they really did turn out to be Builders from Hell.'

'This week we investigate the shoddy firm that put in the hidden cameras we tried to use last week.'

'On *Watchdog* this week, are TV presenters paid too much? No. Goodnight.'

'We've had a problem with our feature, "Why do builders miss deadlines?", so we'll bring you that next week.'

'Tonight we investigate United Dairies, R. Whites and Cadburys in a feature titled, "Milk, milk, lemonade, round the corner chocolate's made."'

'Even though he had taken out a comprehensive funeral care-plan, Navy Seals just dropped his body in the sea.'

'So we wrote to Ryanair to complain about their rudeness and received this letter back: *Dear Dom Littlewood, stick it up yer arse.*'

'I'm Anne Robinson.'
'And I'm Matt Allwright, and coming up, we look at the annoying trend of companies offering you two for the price of one.'

'On tonight's show, we look at a vile con man who keeps returning to dupe the same victim over and over again. And we ask Cheryl Cole why she lets him get away with it.'

'I recently made a purchase from B&Q and found it had a screw loose. It was a packet of loose screws.'

'We received this letter from the Labour Party, complaining that the new Miliband they'd got wasn't anything like as good as the old one.'

84 BAD THINGS TO HEAR IN A

'I can see a head! Get that man out of the way and let me help this pregnant woman.'

'He's a very different colour to his dad, isn't he?'

'This will be the most beautiful moment of your life: screaming and shitting yourself in a paddling pool.'

'You've just circumcised his leg!'

'Clean yourself up and let's go down the pub, I'm gasping.'

'He's not coming out easily. Stand back, I'm going in!'

'Stop screaming! We're trying to film *One Born Every Minute*.'

'Look at the size of that!'

'Whose is the monkey?'

'That's not the afterbirth, that's the baby.'

'What have we here? Let me just put my hand in and ... a bunch of flowers ... the flags of the world ... a white rabbit!'

'Who wants this one?'

'If that's your pancake, where's my placenta?'

'It's a miracle, Mrs Smith – every single one of your husband's sperm has become a baby.'

'We seem to have a spare one …'

'Mind if I take a photo for *National Geographic*?'

'Christ, Mrs Button, the baby looks about ninety-two!'

'OK. Brace! Forceps! Nice to See You, To See You Nice.'

'When I said "caesarean", I didn't mean stab me on the steps of the hospital.'

'Pull!'

MY BROTHER'S A KEEPER

PAUL SHILTON

Corden Bleu: The James Corden Cookbook

Cable Cars: Vince Cable's Great British Motoring Journeys

Twatting Tories by Eric Joyce, MP

Driving Miss Huhne

On the Other Hand, Not a Lot! Tales from Paul Daniels' Shed

Pick a Card, I Can't Do it Myself by Paul Daniels

The Art of Negotiation by Bashar al Assad

Pissed as a Newt: The After-Dinner Anecdotes of Newt Gingrich

Bell End – Warwickshire and England batsman Ian Bell contemplates the end of a long career in cricket

Ewan Whose Army? Ewan McGregor's History of World War II

Great Meals for Under a Fiver by Antony Worrall Thompson

Edward and Mr Simpson: Prince Edward and John Simpson in Conversation

88 UNLIKELY THINGS TO HEAR IN A

'A word about registers: most of the staff are now on one.'

'This term I feel it's important to let the children do exactly what they like and to set their own rules and boundaries. Can I come out now?'

'Miss Grainger is our new French teacher and on behalf of the entire school, I'd like to say, "Ooh-la-la!"'

'A reminder to pupils about the tuck shop – you're not allowed to have plastic surgery until you're sixteen.'

'You're all so fat, from now on running in the corridors is compulsory.'

'This term's French exchange went well; we sent them 4C and they sent us twenty cases of a jolly decent red.'

'There will be no more editions of the school magazine. Our lawyers tell us the title *Barely 16* has already been taken.'

'Someone stole sulphuric acid from the science lab at lunchtime. I want you all to hold your hands out and anyone with their fingers missing will be in detention.'

'And we'll end the day with a cross-country run, which we'll do every day till Tompkins from 4C brings the school bus back.'

'Welcome to this brand-new academy. Quiet everybody, you're only wasting your own time, sponsored by Accurist.'

'Congratulations on everybody achieving an A-star at A-level, which you'll be taking at the end of the year.'

'Now, someone was in the science block at lunchtime and stole the helium canister. Stop that high-pitched giggling at the back.'

'This term we're hoping to completely eradicate bullying from our school. Now please welcome the new boy, Quintin, who does ballet and joins us from a private prep school.'

'Put the sorting hat away, it obviously only works in Hogwarts.'

'The school treasurer is leaving us this term, but with good behaviour might be out in time for Spring term.'

'You remember last year we sadly lost our games teacher. Well, good news, we found him – he'd been buried in the long-jump pit.'

'As it is no longer politically correct to stream the children according to ability, we're now going to be streaming according to skin colour and wealth.'

'Now I know this is a bit of a risk, but, because of cutbacks, this year sex education will be taken by the PE teacher.'

90 *UNLIKELY WEDDING VOWS*

'I take you to be my wife, regardless of the obstacles we may face, such as your penis, Adam's apple and beard.'

'Where you go, I will go, where you stay, I will stay, and your people will be my people. Fuck the restraining order.'

'I love you for your sense of humour and your goodness, but to be honest, it's mainly about the tits.'

'You'll do.'

'From this day forward, forsaking all others unless that ginger bird in the post office breaks up with Steve from the butchers ...'

'I want your love for me to grow like a beautiful flower, which is why I keep watering you and covering you in manure.'

'I take you to be my constant friend, frequent loan guarantor and eternal cover for my homosexuality.'

'Together in times of despair and triumph, although obviously there'll be a lot more of the former.'

'Your God is my God, where you live, I live, and when you die, I will have a very good alibi placing me at least twenty miles away at the time.'

'For better, for worse, for richer, for poorer, for fuck's sake when does the bar open?'

'I take you as my wife in the name of God, my God Thrashtor the Destroyer, merciful lord of the planet Zoob and emperor of the galaxy of the Lizard People.'

'I will love you more with each day, so that after twenty years you might actually give me an erection.'

'I promise not to look at anyone else – yeah, right.'

'I will love you and your mother equally.'

'You can't get better than a Kwik-Fit fitter.'

'Don't go breaking my heart, I won't go breaking your heart.'

'To infinity and beyond!'

'Til death do us part, for richer, for poorer? Hang on, hang on, I didn't agree to this.'

'With this gun, I thee wed …'

'To have and to hold, for richer, for poorer, for as long as I have ze British passport.'

92 *UNLIKELY THINGS TO READ ON*

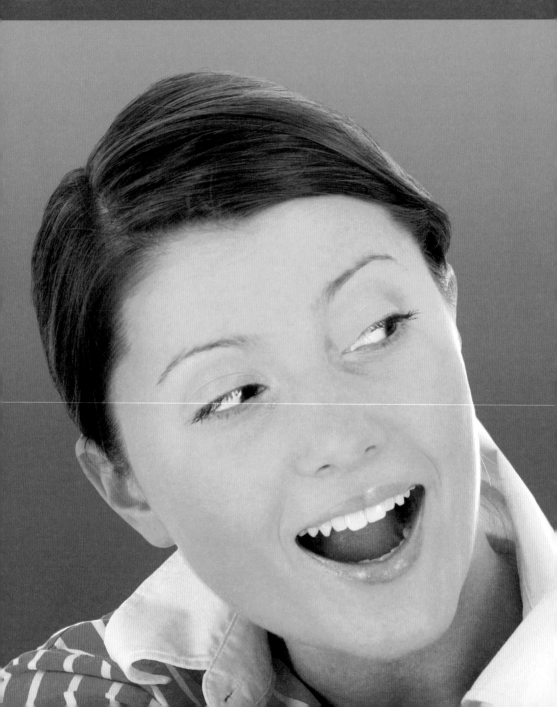

Customers that bought the Coleen Nolan Workout DVD also enjoyed ... masturbating furiously to the Littlewoods underwear catalogue.

Your penis is larger than average, so why not use our herbal shrinking remedy?

We may share your personal details with carefully selected Russian gangsters.

Your Facebook shares have gone up!

If you would like to receive four emails a day, every day, for ever, please click here.

I am an African Banker – I would like to inform you that there is nothing unusual to report.

You look like you're about to write a letter, shall I annoy you?

The problem with Twitter is that just as you're about to say something interesting you realise you've run out of characters just as the message is getting inter–

Your £4.60 bid for Joey Barton has been successful.

Do you want us to store your credit card details for future use? You want to check the box? Really? Check? You're the only one.

94 **UNLIKELY THINGS TO HEAR ON A**

'Our researchers discovered that the scam was organized by Russian gangsters, and at that point they decided maybe it wasn't worth it and perhaps best to drop the matter.'

'Peeling plasterwork and a horrible stench coming from the downstairs plumbing – please welcome Anne Robinson.'

'This man took three days to turn up and service my old boiler. That's the last time I book a male escort for my wife.'

'We want to make sure that the name of this dishonest builder is known by as many people as possible, so we've taken out a superinjunction against him.'

'Not only did the plumber charge £300 an hour, the other workmen urinated into the kitchen sink. But some of them were really hopeless.'

'And there's a happy outcome for Mrs Henderson as the holiday company have agreed to refund the price of her ticket and pay for all her funeral expenses.'

'It was then we at *Rogue Traders* decided to investigate *Builders from Hell* – but they were all out investigating *DIY SOS*.'

'We investigated the *Builders from Hell* and it turned out they were in fact Builders from *Hull*.'

'Of course your Yamaha is making an unfortunate noise – it's an organ, not a motorbike.'

'We did a test and were amazed at just how many useless consumer programmes there were.'

'We would like to warn viewers that the following programme may contain Nicky Campbell.'

'I finally got to speak to the boss of this cowboy hire firm – and he gave me a very good deal on a Stetson, some leather chaps and a lasso.'

'I've managed to get Mrs Smith her money back. But I haven't told her yet, so I'm going to keep it all for myself.'

'A viewer in Cardiff has sent us this postcard about his broadband problems.'

'Are there too many rip-off phone lines? For yes, call 0898...'

- This flat-pack furniture takes two hours, two people and the end of one relationship to build.

- To enjoy this bottled water for longer, just add water.

- Other items you may need to loot: scart lead and plug.

- Do not pull the ripcord till you hit the ground.

- Spare ribs – may contain bones.

- Add boiling water to this Pot Noodle – then flush down lavatory.

- Yorkshire tea – contains EEEEEE-numbers.

- You may now unfasten your seatbelt and start annoying your fellow passengers.

- In case of emergency, break glass, then remove shards of glass from your hand.

- Sword-swallowing kit – contains choking hazard.

- Service-station meat and potato pie. Ingredients: potato.

NOT FOR SALE TO PERSONS UNDER 16

INSTRUCTIONS:
Light blue touchpaper
using safety taper, insert
into duck's arse and stand
well back.

98 SIGNS THAT YOU ARE PAST IT

Your farts just come out as funny little clicking noises.

You fancy the woman in the walk-in bath advert.

You go to see your boss about a rise and he says, 'Didn't you retire four years ago?'.

The only time you laugh out loud is when watching an episode of *Mrs Brown's Boys*.

People ask you to keep the noise down when you get up out of a chair.

Arsenal try to sign you on loan.

Your colleague tells you why you can't open the email he has sent to you, and you can't understand a word he is saying.

You find yourself watching *The Antiques Roadshow*, *Country File* and *Countdown*.

You start buying Werther's Originals.

You agree with things you read in the *Daily Mail*.

People give up their seats for you on public transport.

Not only can you not remember what you came upstairs for, but also whose stairs you have come up and indeed who you are.

You take down numbers of life insurance and will companies.

When you laugh too hard a bit of wee comes out.

You find golf a bit strenuous.

You see a scantily clad young girl in a bar and think, 'She must be freezing.'

Your idea of social networking is advertising for a cleaner in the newsagent's window.

You complain about 'all these young bands with their long hair like Spandau Ballet and Wham'.

You get a designer colostomy bag for your birthday.

All your spam is no longer from Viagra: it is Steradent, Stannah and actual Spam.

100 *BAD THINGS TO SAY IN A JOB*

'Thanks for the job. Just to clarify, I won't have to work with any disabled lesbians, will I?'

'I'm sorry, it's just where I come from we sniff bottoms to greet each other.'

'What will I bring to this job? Well, an empty carrier bag so I can go home with some stationery ...'

'I have no idea if the resumé has got lies on it; as far as I'm concerned, it's the genuine CV of the person whose identity I've stolen.'

'What do you mean everyone has to decide whether I can become prime minister – that's ridiculous.'

'I should say that to overcome my nerves I'm imagining you all naked – and you on the end are looking *good.*'

'I believe I have all the numeracy skills necessary to work on the cash till at Poundland.'

'When you said you wanted to see my curriculum vitae, did you mean tit size?'

'Lets just say, hypothetically, that you found out I was on day release for murder ...'

'Do I have any questions? Yes. How rigorously do you check expenses claims?'

'My best feature is my discretion. In my last job no one ever found out I was shagging the boss's wife.'

'My first question is, will my electronic tag set off the door alarm?'

'Well, I've got two hobbies, really – reading the Koran and Jihad.'

'Where do I see myself in five years? Doing your job or failing that, doing your wife while you're doing your job.'

'I've been interested in banking ever since I discovered that you earn obscene amounts of money no matter how badly you do the job.'

102 UNLIKELY NAMES FOR NEWBORNS

TWATTY

LEMBIT

KICK ME

JEAN-VOLDEMORT

PEGGY-SOUP

WALTER WALQUIM

DWAYNE PIPES

JAN VENEGOOR OF HESSELINK

JOCK STRAP

JENNY TAYLIA

JACK OFF

JOHN-PAUL RINGO

MINNIE KIEV

JOHN THOMAS

WILLIE WANKIE

SUE PERMAN

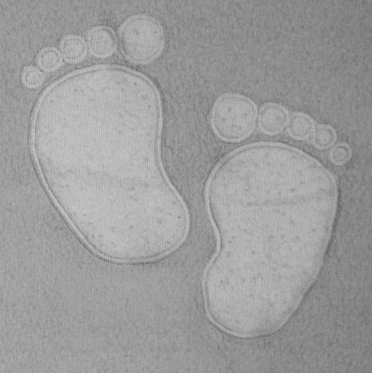

Osama

BAD THINGS TO HEAR IN A

'In an attempt to empathize with my wife, I want you to ram this pineapple up my arse.'

'Fucking hell, there's a little baby coming out of you!'

'We're proud of the level of care the modern NHS affords, Mrs Jones. Now finish your brandy and bite down on this stick.'

'I can definitely see the head! You must remember to fasten your flies, Doctor.'

'Nurse, hot water! I'm gasping for a cuppa.'

'Hold on, Nurse! We're just going to strap a camera to him.'

'Hello!' (Hello!) 'Echo!' (Echo!)

'Has anyone seen my watch? The little bastard's nicked it!'

'Put the baby back in and do it again. The director says we had problems with the mic on that take.'

'Would you like to learn how to change a nappy? I'll just drop my trousers ...'

'She'll be calving any minute now, Mr 'Erriot. You'd better put your wellies on.'

'Thar she blows!'

'Twins! Fetch the she wolf and let's get them suckling.'

'This is a bad time for you to be having a midwife crisis.'

'There, there now, Nurse Death and Nurse Herod will take good care of you.'

'There's a Mr R Stiltskin outside. He says he's come to claim his prize?'

'If you put your ear against it, you can hear the sea!'

'Dr Barrymore is just filling the birthing pool now ...'

'Who chose *Rosemary's Baby* as the birthing DVD?'

Don't read this sign, keep your eyes on the car in fron— Oh shit

Caution, wildlife ahead. (Bits of badger being eaten by birds)

Warning! Long journey ahead – kids in seat behind

You are heading north. Why?

Attention, that last sign about switching to the oncoming lane was a joke – April Fool!

Welcome to Cornwall – here be dragons

Traffic – slow down to an almost complete standstill for three miles, then speed up again for no discernable reason whatsoever

Baby deer crossing road – so speed up and hit a few

Check your tyres – you've just left Liverpool and it's highly likely some of them are missing

Tiredness Kills – take a break. Not now, you idiot – pull over first!

Glastonbury 5 miles – wind up windows now, or risk hearing Coldplay perform.

CABLE & WIRELESS

A LIFETIME OF LISTENING TO THE RADIO

VINCE CABLE

Boyle's Law: The Collected Detective Fiction of Susan Boyle

Pol's Pot: Cambodian Slow-Cooker Recipes

Aung San Suu Kyi's 100 Favourite Daytime Telly Programmes

Portillo Out, Starboard Home: Great British Boat Journeys by Michael Portillo

Any Portillo in a Storm: Michael Portillo, the Autobiography

Marsh Mellow: Meditation the Rodney Marsh Way

Cheese and Pickles: My Love Affair With Food, by Eric Pickles

Straw and Peace: Jack Straw Letters, Volume 1

Clutching at Straws: Jack Straw Letters, Volume 2

The Final Straw: Jack Straw Letters, Volume 3

The Darling Buds of May: Gardening with Theresa

110 *WHAT YOUR PET SAYS ABOUT YOU*

Remember, a dog is for life and not just for Christmas; most other pets, however, can be quietly disposed of by New Year. Here's what your pet says about you:

Staffordshire Bull Terrier: I am a loan shark

Rottweiler: I am a loan shark who has made enough to buy my own pub

Yorkshire Terrier: I'm watching you through my net curtains, young lady

Poodle: I am an elderly homosexual

Jack Russell: I am comfortable in the company of madness

Cat: I am a spinster or a Bond villain or someone who likes having a pet but not having them around much

Pigeons: These are my only real friends since Thatcher closed down t'pit

Snakes: I am a potential serial killer

Rats and Mice: These are not so much pets, more me making the best of a vermin infestation

Panther: I live on the edge of a bleak moorland and enjoy scaring the shit out of sheep and ramblers

Crocodile: I am incredibly stupid and this won't end well

Lion: I'm trying to make my stately home pay

Gerbil: I am very kinky

Horse: My dad feels guilty about leaving Mummy for his secretary

Pony: Will keep spoilt child happy till she marries a banker

Great Dane: Couldn't afford a donkey

Parrot: Lonely old woman or pirate

100 Cats: You smell of wee and actively want to be a cat

Cow: You'd have to be mad. No one has a pet cow. I mean, it's a fucking cow

Mammoth: You are Sir Richard Attenborough in *Jurassic Park*

Fly and Spider: You are an old woman who sleeps with her mouth open

112 *UNLIKELY THINGS TO HEAR FROM*

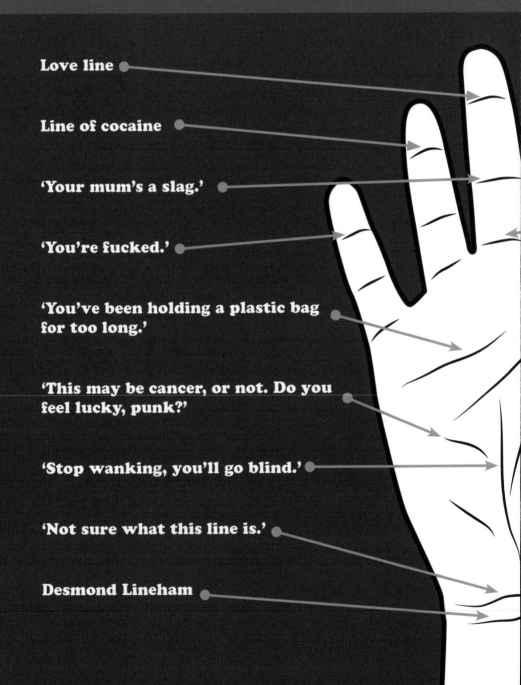

Love line

Line of cocaine

'Your mum's a slag.'

'You're fucked.'

'You've been holding a plastic bag for too long.'

'This may be cancer, or not. Do you feel lucky, punk?'

'Stop wanking, you'll go blind.'

'Not sure what this line is.'

Desmond Lineham

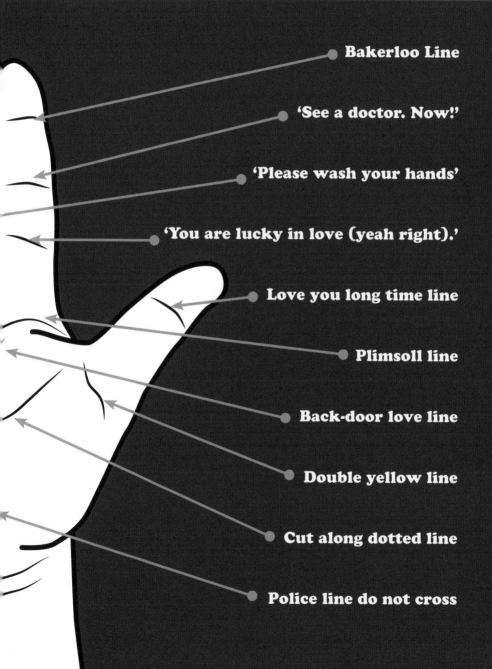

Bakerloo Line

'See a doctor. Now!'

'Please wash your hands'

'You are lucky in love (yeah right).'

Love you long time line

Plimsoll line

Back-door love line

Double yellow line

Cut along dotted line

Police line do not cross

114 *BAD THINGS TO SHOUT DURING*

'Mum!'

'Arrgh! My leg's come loose!'

'Hang on, the phone's ringing.'

'Die!'

'No likey, no lighty!'

'Police!'

'Did you hear that? Did they say
England are 81 for 5?'

'You look just like your sister from here.'

'Geronimo!'

'There's no place like home,
there's no place like home ...'

'Mrs Doubtfire!'

'Fore!'

'Mr Grimsdale!'

'Mein Führer! Schnell! Schnell!'

'Adriaaaaan!'

'Ooh! Heskey, just wide.'

'Prematurus ejaculatus!'

'Is it supposed to do that?'

'On me 'ed, son!'

'Cover your eyes, it's gonna blow!'

'It's a boy!'

116 *UNLIKELY THINGS TO HEAR IN A*

'Here we are, Sir, the cheapest wine, as ordered. Would you like to smell the plastic nozzle on the box?'

'Jamie, do you have ox tongue, or does it just sound like it?'

'I'll have what she's having.'
'An orgasm, Madam? Certainly, follow me.'

'Well, in this restaurant, Sir, Banoffee pie is made with bananas that are off.'

'There's no need for a tip, Sir, we're more than adequately recompensed by our excellent salaries.'

'The dish of the day is salmon, unfortunately the day in question was three weeks ago.'

'Quick – it's Eric Pickles – take down the "All you can eat" sign.'

'Would you mind turning the jazz up, it's not quite loud or annoying enough.'

'This really is a three-star restaurant – the food has been in a freezer for six months.'

'I'm afraid the chef is ill with diarrhoea – but never mind, he left us this Brown Windsor Soup.'

'You'll never believe it, Heston – someone actually likes the liver-flavoured ice cream.'

'The chef will stop serving at nine – he's going somewhere nice to eat.'

'I recommend the Dover Sole – it's a trout I accidentally sat on.'

'It doesn't matter what Mexican food you pick, it's all exactly the same.'

'The chef's surprise, Mr Wallace? He's shagging your wife in the kitchen.'

'With this dish I'd say the house red would take the taste away.'

'The chef is in the kitchen trimming a pair of fatty chops – and when he's finished shaving he'll cook your lunch.'

118 UNLIKELY INSTRUCTIONS

- Hold sheep firmly and enjoy.

- For the first six months of hair transplant, avoid repeated impact such as heading a football.

- Shark-infested waters – do not swim with gaping wound.

- If thrown properly, this should come back to you under its own volition – but please treat your dwarf with respect.

- Caution – the drink the stewardess is about to spill over you is hot.

- Turn left, left again, left again and left again – and you'll be here.

- Shake vigorously. If that fails, try feeding it some breast milk.

- Guts, eyes, anus and scales – all mixed together into a delicious fish paste.

- Slazenger tennis balls (see top of lid for serving suggestion).

- Alphabetti Spaghetti. Warning: contains e-letters.

- Light blue touchpaper using safety taper, stand well back, watch two-second flash and think, 'Thirty quid for that?'

ROOM
SPRAY

Instructions for use:

Spray liberally,
then blame the dog.

ORIGINAL

UNLIKELY EXAM QUESTIONS

Summer 2013

Time allowed: 2 hours 15 minutes

FRENCH EXAM. Candidates are reminded that they will be deducted 10 per cent of their marks if they have washed.

OK, Pathology exam, turn over your body …

Question 1. Stop looking at the bra strap of the girl in front of you.

Translate the Italian for 'Yes'. Is it a) Oui, b) Ja or c) Si?

Explain the world financial crisis with particular reference to chasing a maid down a hotel corridor with your pants down.

HISTORY. Put these events in chronological order: First World War, Second World War.

If Peter Crouch is 6'7" and Abbey Clancy is 5'9", what size box must she stand on to give him oral sex?

MEDIA STUDIES. Explain the term 'superinjunction'. (Remember, you are not permitted to write *anything*.)

SPORTS SCIENCE. Question 1: Are you thick or what?

SOCIOLOGY. Write an essay on the state of the toilets at Glastonbury. Use both sides of the paper.

GEOGRAPHY. Describe how an Oxbow lake is formed in Europe over many millennia due to shifting river courses. Then describe how one is formed in China, in an afternoon, using dynamite and a flooded village.

BIOLOGY. Without singing – what *is* the knee bone connected to?

ENGLISH LITERATURE. Discuss Heathcliff's love for Cathy and ting, innit.

PHYSICS. What is the scientific principle which insists that the invigilator's shoe makes a bizarre squeaking noise every alternate step?

PHILOSOPHY. What does 'Hakuna Matata' mean?

If you are a young offender, please finish the sentence that you are on.

Remember, the French Oral will count towards 20 per cent of your Sex Education GCSE.

The answer to the last question was eleven squared, not eleventy two.

MEDIA STUDIES. If you get an E, how will you take it?

122 BAD THINGS TO SAY IN A JOB

'Anything I'd like to ask you? Errm … what's that thing on your nose?'

'Just one question, really — if I do become a bus driver, do I have to let black people on?'

'I wouldn't shake hands if I were you, I've just been scratching my dick.'

'What's your policy on internet use during office hours? For instance, am I allowed to look at Facebook, eBay and sluttyteenswantcock.com during lunch?'

'When I said on my CV I was "in bread", I've never done any baking — I'm from Norfolk.'

'Yes, I'd like to stand in the forthcoming Libyan elections. My name? Cynthia Gaddafi.'

'Starting on Monday? Hm, I'd actually rather take some of my holiday first.'

'My brother could do the job better but with the help of the unions, I think I could sneak in.'

'My time at Cambridge? Well, it was a long weekend and I recommend the M11 Travel Inn.'

'Thanks for offering me the job of a Saturday boy – now you do know I can't work weekends?'

'Before we offer you the job, Mr Clegg, you do realize none of what you say will ever be listened to?'

'Of course there are one or two lies on my CV – actually, let's save time, I'll show you the true bits.'

'That A-level is not an A-star, that's actually an asterisk; if you look at the bottom it says it was really an E.'

'I can't quite fly a plane yet but I've done that terrorist course, you know, the one where you don't have to take off or land.'

'I've got eight STDs ... sorry, I mean CSEs ... no, I was right first time, STDs.'

124 *GUIDE TO FACIAL HAIR*

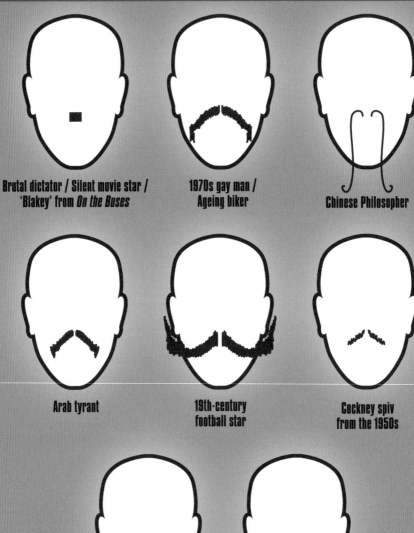

Brutal dictator / Silent movie star /
'Blakey' from *On the Buses*

1970s gay man /
Ageing biker

Chinese Philosopher

Arab tyrant

19th-century
football star

Cockney spiv
from the 1950s

Pussy tickler

Ageing web pervert

15-year-old boy
trying to buy alcohol

Victorian weightlifter /
Weirdo

Middle-aged Welshman
working in haulage

Cartoon villain/Artist

German swinger

Wanker TV producer raising
money for Movember

'The Thinker'

Viking

126 UNLIKELY THINGS TO HEAR FROM

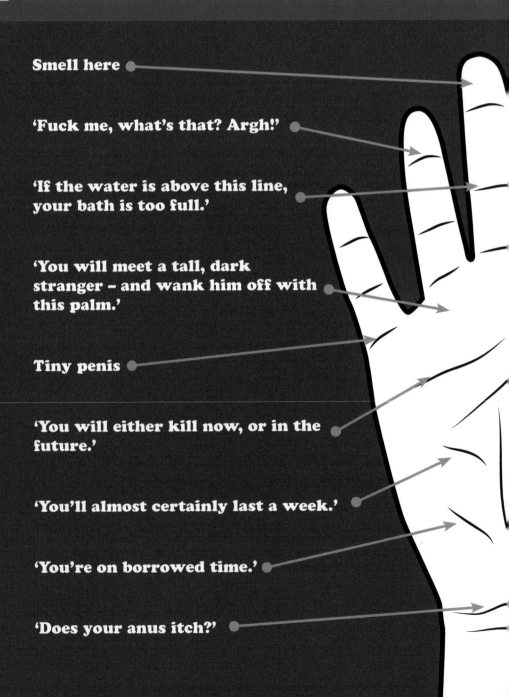

Smell here

'Fuck me, what's that? Argh!'

'If the water is above this line, your bath is too full.'

'You will meet a tall, dark stranger – and wank him off with this palm.'

Tiny penis

'You will either kill now, or in the future.'

'You'll almost certainly last a week.'

'You're on borrowed time.'

'Does your anus itch?'

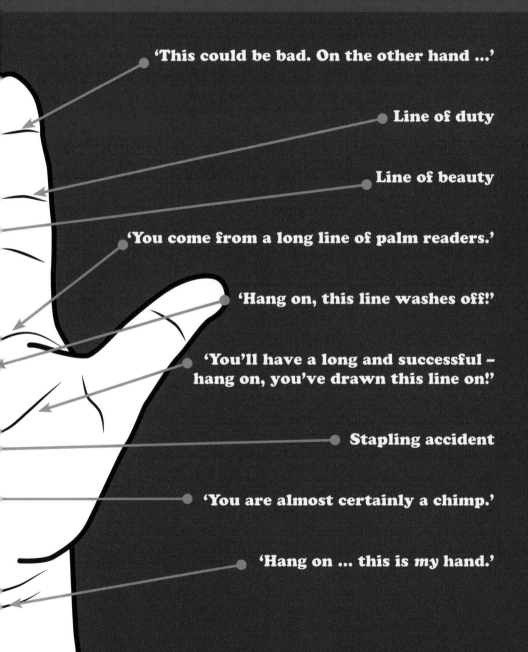

'This could be bad. On the other hand ...'

Line of duty

Line of beauty

'You come from a long line of palm readers.'

'Hang on, this line washes off!'

'You'll have a long and successful –
hang on, you've drawn this line on!'

Stapling accident

'You are almost certainly a chimp.'

'Hang on ... this is *my* hand.'

128 UNLIKELY THINGS TO FIND ON A

Use a blue or black pen

Please note: Everyone filling out the census must first of all return to the town of their birth so that their firstborn can be murdered.

When did you a) come over here
and b) start taking our jobs?

Please list the number of children you have and where in the house you hide from them.

Does my bum look big in this?

How would you describe your job? Fulfilling but deep down you're a bit hurt that no one listens to your ideas?

Please fill in your age and sex. If it's below 30 and female, add what you're wearing.

Do you suffer from Alzheimer's? If yes, go to question 2.
Question 2: Do you suffer from Alzheimer's?

Should Cheryl Cole have been accepted on to American *X Factor*?
Tick box 1 for 'Way aye', or box 2: 'She cannae dinnae'.

List the names of all the people staying in your house tonight – even if it's only Ryan Giggs banging your wife while you waste your time on this.

Did you spill my pint?

Use a blue or black pen

You can fill out this census online. It'll be just as boring but at least there are lights and buttons to press.

If you are in full-time university education, why are you filling this in? You'll get done for TV licence and council tax.

How many people are in your student accommodation? Tick the following boxes:
- [ ] One person per bedroom.
- [ ] Stuart, who's kipping on the sofa while he gets his act together.
- [ ] Hannah, who's saving up to go travelling in order to find herself.
- [ ] Melanie, who got chucked last night but is in the bathroom crying.

How would you describe your religion? Don't put Jedi, you twat. ☐☐☐☐☐

Name. ☐☐☐☐☐   Real name. ☐☐☐☐☐   Oh come on.

How long will you spend filling in this census form:
☐ Under 30 seconds?   ☐ Under 15 seconds?   ☐ Finished?

Where will you be putting this census form:
☐ The bin, ☐ the recycling or ☐ the shredder?

How many men has your wife slept with this year? ☐☐☐☐☐☐☐☐☐☐
And what time do you leave for work? ☐☐☐☐☐

State any disabilities, such as glass eyes or hook hands.

What is your annual income:
☐ Under £40,000, ☐ over £40,000 or ☐ 'Who wants to know?'?

130 *BAD THINGS TO SAY IN A JOB*

'How did I hear about the job? Well, it all started on a bright, cold day in November. I was woken by the deep, rhythmic chimes of the village clock tower and padded gently downstairs. The sun glinted off the roof of the greenhouse as I ...'

'I see you are an equal-opportunities employer, does that mean I've got as much chance as someone who hasn't killed?'

'Oh, when you said you'd like to see my CV, I thought you said cock.'

'Sorry about the smell. Dhansak for lunch.'

'Any questions for you? Yes, is this job something I could do outdoors? Do I need to wear a uniform? Do I use apparatus? I don't know, do the mime again.'

'Hobbies? Most of my spare time is taken up with the dogging.'

'I was down to the last two for Al Qaeda leader last year, but al Zawahiri just had that bit more experience.'

'Yes, I spent a number of years in Cuba ... well, Guantanamo really.

'I would mop up around the school and that, but I could still look at the children, right?'

'I am extremely well qualified to be a school janitor, I have a club foot and a criminal record.'

'Yes, yes, Effendi, I fly plane good.'

'Yes, I'd love to work in your kitchen – but do I have to wash my hands every time I have a shit?'

'Where do I see myself in five years? Probably dead, I've got a highly contagious fatal disease.'

'Why do I want to work in a zoo? Because animals can't tell tales.'

'Where do I see myself in ten years' time? In your job. Which would be a lot more impressive if this wasn't a Burger King.'

'I didn't get you a present, Grandpa. The doctor said you'd be dead.'

'Well, let's see what we get in our monthly payment Christmas club luxury hamper ... Right, beans on toast it is.'

'I love celebrating the birth of our Lord Jesus Christ ... or is it His death? I get so confused.'

'Wow. The new *Mock the Week* book. Just what I wanted.'

'Well, Granny had a good innings. Then had her skull fractured by that nasty bouncer.'

'I know you like wearing that paper-cracker hat, but you really should put on the proper crown for your speech, Ma'am.'

'Here you are, son: a bike. It's a Boris bike, so after the first thirty minutes it'll cost you a pound an hour.'

'Well, next year we know not to use so much brandy on the pudding, but at least the fire brigade managed to save the pets.'

'Brian, when I said serve the neighbours mulled wine with no cloves, I didn't mean for you to be naked.'

'I got plenty of batteries this year, love; you'll be able to pleasure yourself for hours while I go down the pub.'

'Grandad's smoking in the front room, I think we should move him away from the fire.'

'That's all the presents opened, now let's log on to eBay.'

'Your mum's just come round. I'll give her another bottle of Baileys till she passes out again.'

'It's time for *The Great Escape* – let's nip down the pub while your mum's doing the washing up.'

'We've had to cut back at the office party – because the photocopier was repossessed, I've drawn a picture of my arse.'

'This tastes a bit salty. But now I've earned my meal, I'll start with the soup.'

'Welcome back, Madam, and I see you've brought your husband this time.'

'I recommend the cheese board, under one of these table legs, that should stop it wobbling.'

'I recommend the £90 bottle of wine, but then I am on commission.'

'The vegetables are peas and carrots, but most of it is pure vomit.'

'Crunchy on the outside, soft and gooey on the inside; I don't know how that cockroach got in your lunch.'

'Take a deep breath ... and you've had Heston's soup.'

'I knew it was a mistake to bring Bruce Forsyth to this sushi restaurant; he's trying to make me memorize everything on the conveyor belt.'

'Heston, the nitrogen in your ice cream and the glycerine in the fruit combine to … hang on, my stomach's started to rumble.'

'I'm afraid we're out of English wine – we had to unblock the drains.'

'It's okay, Mr Putin, I'll pass on the tea, thank you.'

'I know this is the Hairy Bikers' restaurant, I just don't appreciate finding a pube in my salad.'

'I think it's great that Jamie Oliver's employing young, homeless people, I just don't want them touching my food.'

'Here are your oysters, caviar and champagne, Mr Cameron. How did your "We're all in this together" speech go today?'

'It's French week, so as well as delicious French food, half of our staff are on strike.'

'Tonight we're serving traditional British food – pizza or curry?'

136 BAD THINGS TO SHOUT DURING

'Holy shit!'

'Right, now put your goggles on.'

'We apologize to passengers for
this unscheduled delay.'

'This is all a bit overrated, isn't it?'

'Come on you Spurs!'

'One hundred and EIGHTY!'

'It's Chico time!'

'Higher! Lower! Good game, good game.'

'He's behind you!'

'Damn you, Riddler!'

'I'll have one from the top and
two from the bottom, Carol.'

'Death to the West!'

'Fandabidozeeeeee!'

'I'll get you, Harry Potter!'

'Incoming!'

'Hang on, there's someone in here already!'

'*I'm* Spartacus!'

'Go compare!'

'You will come on my first whistle.
Gladiators ... Ready!'

'The Eagle has landed!'

'What? I never agreed to *that*!'

'Martin Bormann!'

138 BAD THINGS TO SAY IN A JOB

'I have to say, I'm so excited about this job that I'm getting an erection.'

'You sell chicken burgers, do you? I haven't eaten in one of these dumps for years.'

'Where it says I'm a Yale student, I studied key-cutting for three years at Timpson.'

'That machine looks really complicated – can't I just make the customers Nescafé?'

'I hope you're not one of those women who make a great big fuss if someone touches your arse.'

'Let me just clarify what I meant on my CV when I said I'm in ladies underwear …'

'I'm very calm in the workplace, as long as I wear my foil hat and no one touches my computer.'

'Of course I can work with women – don't you worry your pretty little head about that.'

'I don't mind working for the minimum wage, as long as you don't mind me taking a dump in your walk-in fridge.'

'My last job was as a butcher. I was the butcher of Srebrenica.'

'I'm OK with the beard and turban, but I'm not living in a cave for anyone.'

'So, Miss Knox, you were in Perugia for four years. What kept you there?'

'Hello, I'm a woman of child-bearing age.'

'Before I sing a song for you Simon, I'd just like to say all my family are fine and we've got no financial hardships.'

'I understand about equality, I don't stand up when a lady walks into the room but that's usually 'cos I've got a boner.'

UNLIKELY THINGS TO FIND IN A

The sequel to *Tinker Tailor Soldier Spy* – *Einee Meenie Miney Mo*.

'You hold them off while I download the data … Hang on, it won't let me eject the stick. Oh, now it won't let me switch off till it's downloaded an upgrade …'

When it comes to international art-based mysteries, the L.S. Lowry code isn't all it's cracked up to be.

'It's OK, I've set the bomb to go off in five minutes … Oh shit, no, five *months*.'

'Quick, follow that car! Actually, we're on the M25, I'll just walk.'

'Mr Bourne, we've worked out your identity … You're Mr Bourne!'

'What's the code? I don't know. But we've got the rest of the address so the satnav should find it.'

'This man is murdering people according to the Seven Deadly Sins. Here's the plan, seeing as he's already killed five, why don't we just let him kill the other two?'

'He's dead and the only clue as to what happened is a massive empty bottle of hospital anaesthetic and a sheepish-looking doctor.'

He was handed his ticket for Casablanca. He would fly to a small airfield, where he would be met in the middle of the night by a man with a donkey who would take him through a series of rural villages to a tiny guesthouse – the usual easyJet route.

As he reached the edge of the roof, he calculated his escape. A 20-foot jump at a 30-degree angle would carry him the 5 yards he needed to … No, hang on. Is that right? Er, was it 25 feet? Wait. But then they shot him.

After four hours in front of the computer he'd finally done it – he'd got himself an eBay account.

His last shot had to count. If he left any of the ducks standing, he wouldn't win the teddy.

'So we think Jesus had a wife, thanks to this new painting we've discovered by Da Vinci entitled, "Mr and Mrs H Christ at their Wedding".'

He reached for his gun and slowly and methodically filled it up from under the tap.

'This prostitute isn't dead,' said the Norwegian detective, 'she's just pining for the Fjords.'

'My God, we can't keep up with them, they're breaking the new eighty-mile-per-hour speed limit!'

'It's time to weigh the body's brain … Wey-hey!'

142 *UNLIKELY THINGS TO READ ON A*

Due to second sunny day in a row, all roads to the coast are blocked solid

Caution – wide load ahead – Eamonn Holmes on caravanning trip

Caution – school ahead. Speed up now, or you'll look like a perv

Services ahead – last chance to be ripped-off for 25 miles

To save energy these lights have been swit—

Cute blonde in convertible – 500 yards ahead

Kill a child, not your speed ... or is it the other way round? Oh God, I don't know!

Come on, you wuss, you can go faster than that!

Football fans – last chance to moon for ten miles

Accident ahead – you're too busy reading this sign to notice the lorry in front has stopped

Cheap petrol five miles ahead ... fooled you!

144 *UNLIKELY THINGS FOR A TEACHER*

'Morning, thickos.'

'Whoever wrote "Mr Jones suck's cock" on the wall of the gents has appalling grammar.'

'Yeah? Well your mum finds what I'm giving her too hard as well.'

'Of course, GCSEs are piss easy nowadays.'

'OK, now we're going to do today's sex-education class slightly differently. Do you want to say hello to Mr Winkie, boys and girls? He's very shy, you'll have to shout louder than that if you want him to pop out …'

'Do ya feel lucky, punks? Do ya?'

'Here's a letter to take home to your mums and dads. It's about a timeshare I'm running in the Algarve; just get them to pop their bank details on here …'

'Hey, who wants to follow me on Twitter? I'm @Leathergimpmask.'

'OK, well in that case, you'll just have to do the lesson in your underpants. The rest of you open your chemistry textbooks.'

'Today in human biology, we are going to look at rimming, fisting and felching.'

'Now Hitler might have been unpopular, but there's two sides to every story.'

'OK, we're going to be looking at a major historical figure and one of my heroes … former Wolves and England striker Steve Bull.'

'I don't care what that Darwin said. Descended from monkeys?!'

'OK, I think you're pretty prepared for tomorrow's exam, but £10 each would make it a lot easier.'

'It's great to put faces to all the names from the internet site.'

'I have heard a rumour that someone has hacked into the phone of our French student, Edith, and is in possession of photographs of a personal nature. Now, I hardly need to say, if this turns out to be true, I would be very interested in buying some copies.'

'Grasp the shaft firmly like so and then …'

'It's a beautiful day, so we're not just going to have this lesson outside, we're going to have it in the hot tub.'

'Right, I have to pop out during today's metalwork lesson, so connect the blowtorch yourselves, class. If you're messing about when I get back, there'll be trouble.'

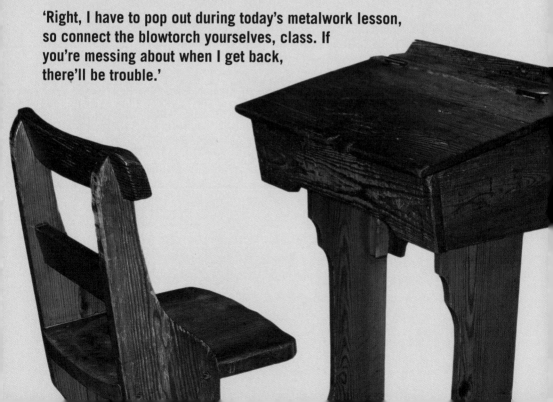

'The Higgs boson has been found … In bed with the Higg's admiral.'

'Darwin's theories are, of course, nonsensical. Sometimes it makes me so angry I want to scoop up my faeces and throw it at him.'

'Joining me to discuss the dangers of GM crops mutating are a physicist, a biologist and a bale of hay.'

'This is dark matter. I trod in it and now I'm trying to get it off my shoe with a stick.'

'Tonight we discuss the mysteries of Pluto. If he's a dog, and Goofy's a dog, how come only one of them can talk and wear clothes?'

'No, that isn't a red dwarf – it's Antony Worrall Thompson.'

'To represent this molecule of DNA, we're going to push Stephen Hawking down this helter-skelter.'

'The gravitational pull is so strong that the pasties have been drawn out of the fridge and are now in orbit around Eamonn Holmes.'

'We used the latest X-ray spectroscopy to see what original sketch lies beneath this masterpiece by Rembrandt. So let's see … oh my god, it's a giant cock and balls!'

'The atoms are bound together by one of the most mysterious forces in the Newtonian universe: Velcro.'

'The universe is ever expanding, until it gets to the size of Angela Merkel's arse.'

'This is incredible! A brand-new species of miniature tiger! Oh no, it's a cat, it's a cat ...'

'400,000 gallons of water a second are coming down this waterfall, which would explain why I desperately need a piss.'

'Ah, the familiar glow of the Northern Lights, the Mancunians have set fire to a car again.'

'Over the years, the female of the species has developed extra layers of blubber to enable survival in the harsh climate of Newcastle city centre on a Friday night.'

'Before I begin the in vitro fertilization of the egg, let me take you out for dinner and buy you a couple of drinks.'

'For Sarah Palin it's conclusive proof that man and dinosaur existed together; for everyone else, *The Flintstones* is just a cartoon.'

'Right, let's just put the pig's head in the microwave and see if the eyes pop out.'

'And if we look through the telescope, there it is, the largest black hole ever seen – hang on, I've left the lens cap on.'

'There's the Great Bear and if we follow that North Star directly downwards – bingo, there's Mrs Richmond at number 48 getting out of the shower.'

148 *UNLIKELY THINGS TO HEAR ON A*

'Welcome to the first episode of our all-male makeover show. Right, sniff that T-shirt. It's alright, isn't it? You're done.'

'So we've transformed overweight and tired-looking Sarah, into overweight and tired-looking Sarah, with a new hat.'

'Yes, she looks ten years younger, so that makes her ... Twelve. Oh.'

'How to look good naked? Buy your husband two bottles of wine.'

'We thought Jenny would look good in ripped jeans, unfortunately they weren't supposed to be ripped around the arse.'

'Gok realized it was a mistake to put her in the shop window naked as they were in Amsterdam.'

'No! It's how to look *good* naked.' (Throws up)

'At the start of the programme she was a hatchet-faced old boot, but sadly we're stuck with the presenter.'

'Next: *Snog Marry Avoid* – yes, we've dramatized Kerry Katona's weekend diary entry.'

'It's always important that collar and cuffs match, so we've died your pubes grey.'

'Welcome to *Snog Marry Avoid*, and here's tonight's contestants: Avoid Avoid Avoid.'

'We took BBC1 and over several years turned it into ITV2.'

'You're going to be getting naked, so a quick word about the watershed. Get yourself behind it so we can't see your fat arse.'

'Now I think I've worked out how to make you look good naked. Pass me that lipstick – I'm going to poke my eyes out.'

'Welcome to the new makeover show – *Pimp My Mum*.'

150 THINGS YOU WOULDN'T WANT TO

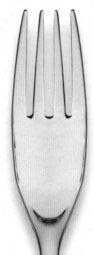

'Ooh, if you're going to have a shit, could you use the upstairs loo? The downstairs can only really deal with piss and pellets.'

'Well darling, I hope these oysters have the desired effect … and you die of food poisoning.'

'Here's the soup – keep your eyes open, I've lost a plaster somewhere.'

'I hope you don't mind – I stuck my cock in the halibut before I put it in the deep frier.'

'What makes you think they're knock-offs? Just have an After Seven Thirty mint and enjoy it.'

'There's a bit of a theme tonight – we're only eating endangered species. Now who's for more panda kebab?'

'Actually there's a funny story behind why I call it jerk chicken …'

'I know it looks like a pizza but it's actually roadkill.'

'You like singing so I've sat you between the twins, John and Edward.'

'Sorry everyone, I think I've burnt this sushi.'

'I've just shat in the soup.'

'When you said it was going to be a banana surprise I didn't think you were going to put it there.'

'Before we start I thought it'd be nice if we just said a few quick words of prayer … to our dark lord, Beelzebub, Master of Hades.'

'I thought we could all eat with our fingers. Now, who's for bolognese?'

'I know you like your meat rare, so I cooked you a white rhino.'

'Who had the chicken? An ambulance is on the way.'

'Before the cheese course we always pass round the smack.'

'Mummy, the tarantula's escaped!'

'You didn't tell anyone you were coming here did you, Salman?'

'No, that's not a rugby injury, his teacher's been buggering him again.'

152 UNLIKELY MEDICAL LABELS

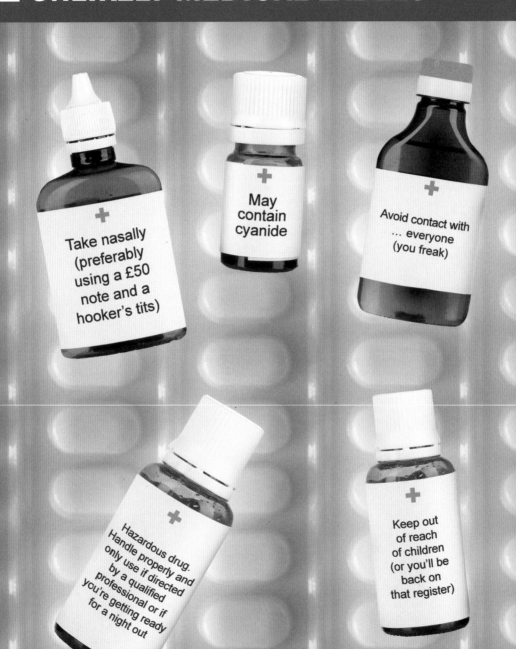

Obesity pills.
See if you can
find room for
four of these a day,
Lard-arse

Take with food. See
inside for serving
suggestion,
recipes and wines
that complement the
Dexmedetomidine

Do not submerge in
water
(unless you are
wearing correct
breathing
apparatus)

Take two
of these every
four hours and
stop
bloody
moaning

154 UNLIKELY THINGS TO HEAR IN A

'It's just that when I ordered the Chocolate Labrador, I thought it would be made of chocolate.'

'Here's your banana surprise, Sir, with a side order of KY jelly.'

'Och, I dinnae understand what this says on the menu: S.A.L.A.D.'

'This is our finest bottle of red, it's £145. Duchy Original ketchup.'

'We've decided not to advertise our restaurant as "child friendly", instead we use the phrase "adult repellent".'

'Yes, you've caught us out there, Sir, the "Light de Angel" *is* Angel Delight.'

'We serve authentic modern Chinese cuisine – it's McDonalds.'

'Mix some basil, pine nuts, olive oil and crème fraîche. Add in some straw and hey pesto!'

'My English is not so good, your chicken tonight is … no sorry, your meal *is* Chicken Tonight.'

'Now who ordered the chicken à la small metal cage kept in incredible pain for it's entire life?'

'Is that garlic foam, or have you just coughed on my plate?'

'I think you're confusing your Petit Chablis with the Pouilly-Fumé. Nonetheless, here, as ordered is the Petit Filous. And a teaspoon.'

'This is "fusion" food, Sir, it's disappointing *and* expensive.'

'Good news about your steak, Sir – I managed to wrestle it back off the dog.'

'May I recommend the Chablis, Sir; that should get her drunk enough to sleep with you.'

'Mm, that's an unusual taste. What exactly is in the "Death by Chocolate"?'

156 *UNLIKELY THINGS TO FIND IN A*

'Sadly I went to a cheaper tattoo parlour, so I'm starring in *Girl with a sort of long lizard thing, with a sort of blobby head tattoo*.'

The bullet was heading straight for his heart but was deflected by his cigarette case ... right into his brain.

'If I can't work out what these thirty-nine steps are I'm definitely going to be kicked out of *Strictly Come Dancing* this week!'

'Any clues, Sergeant?'
'No, Sir – the man at the motel who dresses in his dead mother's skin says he didn't see anything.'

'It's not the Triffids I'm worried about – have you seen the size of the greenfly?'

Ed Miliband eased open the buff file and started to read ... This was dynamite, he lisped, his adenoids trembling with excitement.

'Check the deceased's emails. He must have bought a penis enlargement kit. Otherwise we wouldn't have run out of chalk.'

There in the briefcase was a million pounds in used notes. That could mean only one thing – the World Cup was going to Qatar.

'Perhaps the victim's emails will give us a clue as to the murderer. It's either a Nigerian prince or the manufacturers of herbal Viagra.'

'Is that a gun in your pocket, or are you just pleased to see me?' she purred.
'It IS a gun,' he replied, 'and I've just shot my cock off.'

'Alright,' said the Icelandic detective, 'I'll have this case solved by sunset.' And sure enough, six months later, he had.

It was his most baffling case ever. She'd had an accident at work that wasn't her fault and if he didn't win, he wouldn't get a fee.

The victim was showing signs of major trauma but there were no signs of injury. 'Get up,' said the referee.

He fired the colt at the window, and with a shriek, the young pony flew through the air and smashed into the glass.

'Do you have the girl? Let me see her.'
'Not until you give us the money.'
'Alright, but this is the last time I use Russian Brides.com'

'The suspect has gone into a screening of *Avatar*, we'll go in in ten minutes when he's asleep.'

He carefully filled the magazine – well, the toilet was occupied and he had nowhere else to go.

He gave himself away as he attempted to unscrew the red-hot silencer.

158 UNLIKELY THINGS TO READ ON A

Kids with concrete on bridge ahead

Next petrol £1.51 a litre ... £1.52 ... £1.53 ... £1.54

Motorway services ahead – we buy roadkill

Caution, debris in road ahead, mainly consisting of the last car that didn't take the 'debris in road ahead' sign seriously

M3 closed Junction 4, M4 closed Junction 3. Something like that, anyway

Next Exit – last chance to buy family-sized bags of crisps, garden furniture and hits played on pan pipes, for fifty miles.

Coming up ahead, motorway goes down to two lanes for a bit. Don't ask me why, it just does.

Testing, Testing: the quick brown fox jumped over the lazy dog.

Caution! Susan Boyle ahead, by which I mean, the Glasgow turn-off ahead.

Level Crossing Ahead. Put your foot down and you might just make it, or are you some sort of chicken?

160 UNLIKELY THINGS TO HEAR YOUR FLATMATE SAY

'That girl you met last night is coming round; you're going to have to hit her with the shovel again.'

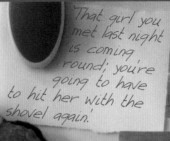

'Of course I'm not dressing a bit like you. I'm dressing exactly like you, these are your clothes.'

'Guess what colour I've just left the toilet bowl: red or black?'

'It's a funny story, you'll laugh at this. So I ordered an Escort girl just before your mum came round...'

'Two things - we've run out of toilet paper, and also you might want to wash your towels.'

'There are twenty-four Latvians in the caravan but you won't know they're there.'

'No, no, no. We'll chop him up in the bath, then bury him.'

'My headache's cleared up, but I do feel a bit mental today.'

'You just have to initial the box. You don't have to initial every single cornflake.'

'I hope you don't mind, I borrowed one of your Ryvitas. I needed a snack after I had a wank in your underwear drawer.'

'It's fine, I've flushed it, you can go in straightaway.'